浙江省普通本科高校"十四五"重点教材

高等院校经济管理类专业"互联网+"创新规划教材

# MANAGEMENT AND ORGANIZATION
## Bilingual Teaching Case

# 管理与组织
# 双语教学案例

主　编　彭新敏　钱树静
副主编　陈士慧　吴　瑶　国维潇

北京大学出版社
PEKING UNIVERSITY PRESS

## 内 容 简 介

本书以 15 家中国企业的管理实践来解释管理理论，阐述了计划、组织、领导与控制四大基本管理职能，涵盖了管理与组织的基本知识。本书中的每个案例均包含案例正文、案例问题和分析提示三部分内容。本书一方面可以使国外学生对中国企业的管理方法与管理实践有直观的认识；另一方面也可以满足国内高校进行双语或全英文教学的需要。

本书适合作为高等院校管理学课程的配套教材，也适合作为企业管理培训用书和自学参考书。

**图书在版编目（CIP）数据**

管理与组织：双语教学案例 / 彭新敏，钱树静主编．—北京：北京大学出版社，2023.6
高等院校经济管理类专业"互联网+"创新规划教材
ISBN 978-7-301-33638-0

Ⅰ．①管… Ⅱ．①彭…②钱… Ⅲ．①组织管理学—双语教学—教案（教育）—高等学校 Ⅳ．①C936

中国版本图书馆 CIP 数据核字（2022）第 233051 号

| | |
|---|---|
| **书　　　名** | 管理与组织：双语教学案例<br>GUANLI YU ZUZHI: SHUANGYU JIAOXUE ANLI |
| **著作责任者** | 彭新敏　钱树静　主编 |
| **策 划 编 辑** | 李娉婷 |
| **责 任 编 辑** | 耿　哲　陶鹏旭 |
| **数 字 编 辑** | 金常伟 |
| **标 准 书 号** | ISBN 978-7-301-33638-0 |
| **出 版 发 行** | 北京大学出版社 |
| **地　　　址** | 北京市海淀区成府路 205 号　100871 |
| **网　　　址** | http://www.pup.cn　新浪微博:@北京大学出版社 |
| **电 子 信 箱** | pup_6@163.com |
| **电　　　话** | 邮购部 010-62752015　发行部 010-62750672　编辑部 010-62750667 |
| **印 刷 者** | 河北文福旺印刷有限公司 |
| **经 销 者** | 新华书店 |
| | 787 毫米 × 1092 毫米　16 开本　14.75 印张　220 千字<br>2023 年 6 月第 1 版　2023 年 6 月第 1 次印刷 |
| **定　　价** | 48.00 元 |

未经许可，不得以任何方式复制或抄袭本书之部分或全部内容。
**版权所有，侵权必究**
举报电话: 010-62752024　电子信箱: fd@pup.pku.edu.cn
图书如有印装质量问题，请与出版部联系，电话: 010-62756370

# 前　言

经过四十多年的改革开放，中国一大批企业迅速崛起并进入全球市场，它们不仅成为行业领先者，也创造了先进的管理模式，吸引了越来越多的国外学生来学习中国企业的管理方法与最新实践。本书以党的二十大报告提出的"完善中国特色现代企业制度，弘扬企业家精神，加快建设世界一流企业"等精神为指引，力求讲好中国企业创新创业故事，传播好中国特色管理理论与实践。

"管理与组织"是工商管理类专业的学科基础课，具有基础性、综合性等特点。本书以 15 家中国企业的管理实践来阐明管理学基础知识。通过管理实践案例来解释管理理论，可以丰富教学内容，提升教学效果。本书配有中英文版本，一方面可以让来华留学生对中国领先企业的管理实践有直观的认识；另一方面也可以满足国内高校双语或全英文教学的需要。因此，本书适合作为高等院校管理学课程的配套教材，也适合作为企业管理培训用书和自学参考书。

本书包含 15 个中国企业案例，主要讲述了管理的四大基本职能——计划、组织、领导与控制，涵盖了管理理论的主要知识点。案例 1 主要解释管理者角色和管理职能理论，案例 2 研究的是组织文化的形成与影响，案例 3 研究的是外部环境对企业管理的影响，案例 4 研究的是企业的绿色管理，案例 5 研究的是企业社会责任，案例 6 研究的是管理者决策知识，案例 7 研究的是企业计划制订与目标设置，案例 8 研究的是计划职能中的战略管理，案例 9 研究的是组织职能中的组织结构设计，案例 10 和案例 11 研究的是领导职能中的人力资源管理，案例 12 研究的是创业团队管理，案例 13 和案例 14 研究的是领导理论和员工激励，案例 15 研究的是控制职能。每个案例均包含案例正文、案例问题和分析提示。案例正文主要讲述案例企业的管理与决策过程；案例问题的设置是希望学生带着问题去阅读案例；分析提示是启发学生可以结合哪种管理理论，从哪些维度对案例进行分析。

本书的编者都是来自宁波大学商学院的教师，具体分工如下：案例 1～7 由彭新敏编写，案例 13 由钱树静编写，案例 8、10、11、12、14、15 由陈士慧编写，案例 9 由吴瑶编写；本书案例 10～14 的在线视频由国维潇拍摄，案例 9 的在线视频由吴瑶拍摄，案例 1～8 和案例 15 的在线视频由钱树静拍摄，并由钱树静负责课程资源建设与维护；全书由彭新敏统稿。本书配套的在线课程资源详见 https://www.xueyinonline.com/detail/222544788。

本书的顺利出版得益于宁波大学工商管理国际化专业建设项目的支持。在本书的编写过程中，宁波大学硕士研究生史慧敏、王昕冉、韩文泽、马帅、冯伟绩、郑碧婷、何周丽、石婧、郑梅园、倪嘉婕做了大量的资料收集与整理工作，北京大学出版社做了耐心细致的编辑工作，在此一并表示感谢！

由于编者水平有限，本书如有不足之处，恳请同行、读者批评指正！

彭新敏

宁波大学

2023 年 1 月

【资源索引】

# Preface

After 40 years' rapid development since China's reform and opening up policy, many Chinese companies have integrated into the global market and become industry leaders, creating advanced management patterns and attracting more and more foreign students to study these management concepts and innovative practices. This book upholds the spirit put forward in the 20th National Congress of the Communist Party of China, which emphasizes "improving the modern corporate system with distinctive Chinese features, encouraging entrepreneurship, and moving faster to help Chinese companies become world-class outfits". This book aims to share compelling stories of innovation and entrepreneurship in Chinese enterprises while disseminating Chinese management theories and practices that are uniquely tailored to the local context.

As one of the fundamental courses for business administration and related subjects, Management and Organization is a basic and comprehensive course. In this book, the management practices of 15 Chinese companies are selected to explain the fundamental knowledge in management. The management theories are explained through the management practices, which makes the teaching more extensive and effective. This book is drafted in both Chinese and English, which could not only help foreign students in China to get an intuitive understanding of the management practices of the leading Chinese companies, but also adapt to the trends of bilingual or English teaching in Chinese universities and colleges. Therefore, this book may be taken as supporting teaching materials for management courses in universities and colleges, as well as a reference for enterprise training and self-study.

This book takes the management practices of 15 Chinese companies as cases to explain the 4 basic functions of management (planning, organizing, leading, and controlling) and reflect the main knowledge points of management theories. Case 1 mainly describes the roles and skills of the managers. Case 2 discusses the formation of organizational culture and its influences. Case 3 discusses the external environment's influences on corporate management. Case 4 discusses the green management of corporate. Case 5 is about corporate social responsibility and business ethics. Case 6 explains the knowledge of managers' decision-making. Case 7 is about plan-making and objective-setting of a corporate. Case 8 is about strategic management in the function of planning. Case 9 discusses the design of organization structure in the function of organizing. Case 10 and Case 11 are about HR management in the function of leading. Case 12 is about the management of entrepreneurial teams. Case 13 and Case 14 are about leadership theories and employee motivation. Case 15 is about the controlling function. Each case is divided into three parts: case description, case questions, and tips for answering the questions. Case description mainly describes the management and decision-making processes of the company. Case questions are set to hope the students read the case by keeping the questions in mind. Tips for answering the questions tell the students which management theories and dimensions they can refer to when analyzing the cases.

All writers participating in this book are teachers from the School of Business of Ningbo University. In particular, Case 1～7 are written by Peng Xinmin, Case 13 is written by Qian Shujing, Case 8, Case 10, Case 11, Case 12, Case 14 and Case 15 are written by Chen Shihui, Case 9 is written by Wu Yao. The online videos for Case 10～14 of this book were filmed by Guo Weixiao, the online video for Case 9 was filmed by Wu Yao, the online videos for Case 1～8 and Case 15 were filmed by Qian Shujing, who is also responsible for the development and maintenance of the course resources. This book is finally compiled and edited by Peng Xinmin. For detailed online course resources related to this book, please visit https://www.xueyinonline.com/detail/222544788.

The successful publication of this book was made possible with the support of the Business Administration Internationalization Program of Ningbo University. Several postgraduates from Ningbo University did lots of data collection and sorting work, including Shi Huimin, Wang Xinran, Han Wenze, Ma Shuai, Feng Weiji, Zheng Biting, He Zhouli, Shi Jing, Zheng Meiyuan and Ni Jiajie. Peking University Press provided patient and meticulous editing work, for which I express my deep gratitude.

Inadequacy and deficiencies are inevitable due to limited abilities of the writers. Any criticism and suggestions from peers and readers are appreciated.

Peng Xinmin<br>
Ningbo University<br>
January 2023

# 目　　录

案例 1　舜宇的管理之道 ............................................................. 1

案例 2　永新光学的企业文化 ....................................................... 9

案例 3　数益工联助力制造业数字化转型 ................................... 15

案例 4　青山的绿色管理 ............................................................. 23

案例 5　天港公益基金的"橙计划" ............................................. 29

案例 6　缸鸭狗的传承与创新 ..................................................... 35

案例 7　宁波慈星的新产品开发 ................................................. 43

案例 8　海伦钢琴的转型升级 ..................................................... 51

案例 9　风华的组织结构变革 ..................................................... 59

案例 10　恩凯的人力资源管理 ................................................... 67

案例 11　忘不了服饰的领导实践 ............................................... 73

案例 12　立拓能源的创业团队 ................................................... 79

案例 13　宁波海辰大药店的店长激励 ....................................... 85

案例 14　京博的领导实践 ........................................................... 91

案例 15　捷丰的控制管理 ........................................................... 97

| Case | Title | Page |
|---|---|---|
| Case 1 | Management Key of Sunny | 103 |
| Case 2 | Corporate Culture of Novel Optics | 113 |
| Case 3 | SHUYILINK Empowers the Manufacturing Industry's Digital Transformation | 121 |
| Case 4 | Green Management Practices of Tsingshan | 129 |
| Case 5 | "Orange Initiative" of Teckon Foundation | 137 |
| Case 6 | Inheritance and Innovation of Gang Ya Gou | 145 |
| Case 7 | New Product Development at Ningbo Cixing | 155 |
| Case 8 | The Transformation and Upgrading Process of Hailun Piano | 165 |
| Case 9 | Fenghua's Organizational Restructuring | 173 |
| Case 10 | HR Management of NKM | 181 |
| Case 11 | Leadership Practices in Wonbly | 189 |
| Case 12 | Entrepreneurial Team of Lituo Energy | 197 |
| Case 13 | The Motivation for Store Managers at Ningbo Haichen Pharmacy | 205 |
| Case 14 | Leadership Practices of Chambroad | 213 |
| Case 15 | JF's Control and Management Practice | 221 |

# 案例 1

## 舜宇的管理之道

## 【案例正文】

1984年，舜宇光学科技（集团）有限公司（以下简称舜宇）在浙江省余姚市成立，它是全球领先的综合光学零件及产品制造商。舜宇于2007年6月在香港联交所主板上市。舜宇专业从事光学及光电相关产品的设计、研发、生产及销售，其主要产品包括三大类：一是光学零组件，主要包括玻璃/塑料镜片、平面产品、手机镜头、车载镜头、安防监控镜头及其他各种镜头；二是光电产品，主要包括手机摄像模组、3D光电模组、车载模组及其他光电模组；三是光学仪器，主要包括显微镜及智能检测设备等。目前，舜宇已经形成了手机、汽车、安防、显微仪器、机器人、AR/VR、工业检测、医疗检测八大事业板块。

从当年的一家没钱、没人、没技术的"三没"企业发展为今天的光电行业之星，舜宇的成长离不开其创始人王文鉴的领导。王文鉴认为：一家企业要想在激烈的市场竞争中取胜，管理层必须根据企业内外部环境的变化，及时对企业生产经营作出正确的决策；在遇到市场环境发生变化或者出现突发事件时，管理层要及时进行管控，寻找出相应的解决措施，只有这样，才能带领企业获得成功。

### 1. 光学元件加工起步

1983年，为了培养优秀技术骨干，浙江省余姚市城北公社与浙江大学光仪厂签订协议，派出部分人员前往浙江大学光仪厂学习光学冷加工技术，由当时余姚电容电器厂的质检员王文鉴带队。1984年11月，学成归来的王文鉴带着8名高中毕业生及6万元贷款创办了舜宇的前身——余姚第二光学仪器厂（以下简称光仪厂）。但由于当时全国光学行业不景气，原本谈妥的为浙江大学光仪厂提供加工业务的合作落了空。能否获得加工业务成为光仪厂能否生存下去的首要问题。在这个关键时刻，王文鉴以杭州照相机械研究所提供的信息为依据，预测照相机将随着人们物质生活水平的改善而成为畅销产品。恰逢光仪厂又具备生产照相机镜头的能力，这就为其跻身照相机镜头生产行列提供了难得的契机。于是，舜宇决定为浙江照相机一厂生产海燕Ⅰ型相机镜头。现在看来，这一决策是成功的。

**2. 横向联营扩大生产**

1986年下半年，王文鉴与管理层在进行了认真细致的沟通后，决定与相机大厂实行横向联营，壮大自身实力，从而使企业得到迅速发展。王文鉴认为：一方面，职工的技术素质通过几年的教育培训已经有了很大提高，光仪厂的生产能力也在不断提高；但另一方面，主要供货单位浙江照相机一厂的销量呈下滑趋势，这使得舜宇的生产又一次面临危机。形势迫使舜宇寻找新的出路，在进行市场调查的过程中，杭州照相机械研究所的李康主任给王文鉴带来一个重要消息——天津照相机厂计划扩大生产，并打算在全国范围内寻找能为他们生产配套镜片镜头的企业。于是，王文鉴抓住机会，立即向天津照相机厂表达了想为其生产东方S4相机镜头的愿望。当时的舜宇才刚起步，知名度不高，想和国内顶尖照相机企业建立合作简直是无法想象的。在天津照相机厂派代表来舜宇考察期间，王文鉴要求员工做好充分准备，并请来了余姚市领导为其助阵，充分表现出舜宇对此次合作的诚意与决心。最终，天津照相机厂代表被王文鉴所带领的团队的"四千"精神（走遍千山万水，说尽千言万语，想尽千方百计，吃尽千辛万苦）所打动，答应给舜宇一次尝试的机会，但舜宇必须在75天内完成1000套合格镜片的交货任务。当时舜宇面临的竞争对手还有南京一家老牌的军工企业以及上海南汇光仪厂，其压力非常大。

为了完成这次任务，王文鉴依托已有的人脉，将胶木厂的仓库作为舜宇的生产车间，并聘请江西光学仪器厂的老师傅用新的工艺技术进行样品试制。为达到产品加工要求，王文鉴从北京一家已停产的日资企业购买了一台二手精磨和抛光设备，还对各个部门进行了精确分工，鼓励全体员工要有信心完成这项任务。经过了70多天的努力，舜宇准时完成了1000套镜片的交货任务。为了保险起见，王文鉴还请了专业人员对1000套镜片进行认真细致的检验。最终，镜片质量全部合格，并在约定时间内送到天津照相机厂，而此时其他两家公司还未完工。

1987年，舜宇与天津照相机厂签订了联营合同书，舜宇与天津照相机厂的合作由原先的一般加工合作变成了更紧密的配套生产合作。在配套生产过程中，为进一步提高生产效率，舜宇引进了国家重点科研项目成果并对其进行技术改造，这一举动大大提高了舜宇的技术能力。在合作的过程中，舜宇还从天津照相机厂获得了更为先进的生产工艺，从而使得舜宇的生产效率远远超过了当时国内的许多大厂。经过短短一年时间的联营，舜宇的产值从原先的51.29万元直接增至321.36万元，利润由原先的13.14万元增至46.34万元，为天津照相机厂生产的镜片增至10万套。

**3. 不断拓展市场边界**

20世纪90年代，随着科学技术的不断发展，光学技术被越来越多的行业所需要，光学行业的生产厂商数量不断增加，中国光学市场的竞争也日趋激烈。此时，舜宇了解到国外对中低档镜头及镜片的需求与日俱增。

王文鉴在1988年下半年提出了"两个转变"战略，即由单一的国内市场转变为国内、国际市场并举，以及由单一的元件加工转变为元件加工、整机生产并举。但是在那个年代同外商做生意并不容易，外商对产品的质量要求高，给的价格却低。最为关键的是在那个年代外商掌握着交易的主动权，对于谈好的交易，外商说取消就取消，生产厂商只能自己承担交易失败的风险。

对舜宇而言，产品要进入国际市场，原来"按图生产"的方式显然不能满足外商的需求，必须根据外商提供的技术参数，由专家设计图纸，然后才能生产。舜宇要在短时间内培养出这方面的人才显然是不现实的，但是若能与浙江大学合作，它就可以借助浙江大学的研发力量使自己的产品快速地进入国际市场。对浙江大学而言，拥有好的技术却没有生产能力也是其痛点。于是，舜宇与浙江大学光电技术开发公司组成联营公司，以"浙江大学设计、舜宇生产"的模式进行合作生产。随着联营合作的深入，以及为适应建立现代企业制度的需要，1994年联营公司改组为浙江大学余姚光电（集团）股份有限公司。

此后，舜宇的市场逐渐拓展至美国、加拿大等国家。比如，美国的POC公司将舜宇生产的各类镜头和光学元件列入了供应商目录。

**4. "名配角"战略的成功**

2003年,王文鉴认真分析了国内外的宏观经济环境,剖析了舜宇自身的发展现状,正式提出了"名配角"战略。第一,服务"名主角"(指具有全球影响力和知名度的国际光电产业公司),"配角"与"主角"可以结成战略合作伙伴;第二,"配角"自身要有很高的知名度和美誉度,在全球范围内拥有影响力。

王文鉴判断手机摄像模组未来将往高像素方向发展,原有的CSP(Chip Scale Package,芯片级封装)工艺无法满足未来的需求,因此他提前组建相关团队,购置相关设备,筹建COB(Chips on Board,板上芯片封装)生产线。从市场应用的角度来讲,CSP主要用于800万像素及以下的领域;COB则可用于800万像素以上的领域,只是设备的投入资金更多。COB生产线投产后,曾一度遇到高像素市场需求停滞的情况,直到2010年高像素市场才开始出现爆发式增长,舜宇得以"弯道超车",嵌入多家知名手机厂商的供应链,成为智能手机领域首屈一指的供应商。

多年的"名配角"战略不仅使舜宇的发展重新回到了高速增长的轨道上,而且使舜宇成功地保持了这种强劲的增长态势,舜宇的销售收入从2004年的4亿元增至2020年的380亿元,增长了94倍。

回顾舜宇的发展历程可以发现,从最初的相机镜头加工到复杂的光学仪器生产,再到如今高精尖的手机摄像模组生产,创始人王文鉴总是在关键时刻作出正确决策,从而成功地带领舜宇从一家名不见经传的乡镇企业发展为世界领先的综合光学产品制造商。

**【案例来源】**

陈晓平."名配角"舜宇[J].21世纪商业评论,2020(4):60-63.

彭新敏,祝学伟.绿叶亦有芬芳时:"名配角"舜宇的崛起之路[J].清华管理评论,2020(10):134-140.

彭新敏,祝学伟.机会窗口、联盟组合与后发企业的技术赶超:舜宇1984—2018年纵向案例研究[J].南开管理评论,2022,25(4):70-78.

仝彤. 双元性学习视角下后发企业技术创新研究：以宁波市 S 集团为例 [J]. 改革与开放，2020（Z3）：18-22.

谢钱，周晓青. 王文鉴：中国智能光学制造先行者——中国 500 强民企舜宇集团的腾飞秘诀 [J]. 企业研究，2016（12）：32-41.

## 【案例问题】

1. 随着舜宇的发展，创始人王文鉴的管理角色发生了什么样的变化？

2. 在舜宇不同的发展阶段，创始人王文鉴分别展现了哪些管理技能？他是如何有效行使管理职能的？

## 【分析提示】

1. 根据王文鉴在舜宇发展过程中所制定的决策的变化，运用管理者角色理论，对其在组织中的角色进行分析。

2. 根据王文鉴对舜宇在发展过程中所面临的难题的解决对策，运用管理者技能理论和管理职能理论，说明管理者的技能是如何随着企业的发展而不断变化的，以及管理者是如何执行计划、组织、领导与控制四大管理职能的。

【管理者做什么？】

案例 2

永新光学的企业文化

## 【案例正文】

宁波永新光学股份有限公司（以下简称永新光学）成立于1997年，现位于浙江省宁波市高新区，是一家专业生产显微镜和光学元件的光学企业。永新光学拥有NOVEL、NEXCOPE、江南等自主品牌，年产十万余台光学显微镜和数千万件光学元件，是徕卡、蔡司、尼康等多家国际知名企业的核心供应商。2017年，永新光学凭借其光学显微镜产品入选国家制造业单项冠军培育企业。2019年，永新光学主导编制了国际标准ISO 9345：2019《显微镜成像系统和成像部件的连接尺寸要求》，同年永新光学获国家技术发明二等奖。2021年，永新光学成功通过复评升级为国家制造业单项冠军示范企业。

永新光学能够从最初生产功能单一的低端显微镜发展到为"嫦娥"工程制造多款光学镜头，从只能加工光学元件的小企业成长为光学显微镜行业的领先企业，根源在于其"至诚至善、求是创新"的核心价值观。自成立之初，永新光学的企业文化就激励着每一位员工。

### 1. 永新光学创立

曹光彪先生祖籍宁波，是中国知名的企业家，宁波帮商圈的代表人物，被誉为"世界毛纤大王"。怀抱着科教兴国的愿望，曹光彪于1997年投资了宁波光学仪器厂，该厂改制后成为宁波永新光学股份有限公司。曹光彪认为，强国之路的必然要求是发展国之重器，这也成了永新光学的不懈追求。

1997年，浙江大学迎来了百年校庆，昔日学子纷纷返回母校，曹光彪也参加了此次校庆。校庆期间，曹光彪请浙江大学光学系的导师们帮他推荐一位既懂技术又具有国际化视野的管理者来管理永新光学。当时，光学系的多位导师都推荐了毛磊。曹光彪的个人魅力以及他对中国光学未来的发展期望打动了毛磊，令毛磊对永新光学未来的发展充满信心。毛磊当即决定接受挑战，成为永新光学的总经理兼总工程师。

在将公司指挥权移交给毛磊的时候，曹光彪只说了一个原则：无论如何改革，都不可辞退任何一个员工，要善待员工。1997年的永新光学面临着诸多难题：产品结构单一、质量水平较低，老员工和退休员工较多，工人因劳资纠纷罢工，等等。管理层在讨论后一致认为，在不辞退任何一名员工的前提下，只有开发出利润相对较高的中高档生物显微镜和光学元件，把产品销往欧美等发达国家，才能获得生存空间。当时，恰逢摩托罗拉公司的采购总监到中国寻找生产光学激光读取镜头的合作厂商，并发现了永新光学。永新光学上下都十分重视，根据客户对产品的加工要求，工厂技术工程师熬了几个通宵进行产品与工艺设计，最终设计出令摩托罗拉满意的方案，双方当即签下一笔价值几百万元的合同。此次合作帮助永新光学度过了危机。

随后，永新光学加大了与行业领先企业的合作力度，并开始与尼康、徕卡等国际领先企业合作。由于显微镜和光学元件具有高精度、多品种、小批量的特点，因此合作的形式主要是"以销定产"，即根据客户的需求提供产品制造的工艺方案，并进行加工生产。永新光学在这样的合作模式下与客户保持着密切的联系，订单数量逐年增多，永新光学不仅获得了充裕的资金，还实现了生产工艺的稳步提升。

**2. 产学研合作**

2010年，嫦娥二号人造卫星顺利升空，卫星上的监控相机镜头是由永新光学与浙江大学花费五年时间联合研制出来的。这支镜头品质极高，它在保证拍摄画面质量的同时，还要承受火箭起飞时的加速度和月球表面恶劣的外部环境。该监控相机镜头的开发，不仅提高了永新光学的研发能力，还提升了其社会责任感和使命感。2013年，永新光学再次与浙江大学联手，为嫦娥三号研制了降落相机镜头。

嫦娥二号、嫦娥三号卫星上的相机镜头的成功研制，拓展了永新光学与各大知名高校合作的广度和深度。例如，永新光学先后与清华大学、宁波大学等高校建立了合作关系，它还与浙江大学签订了硕士研究生联合培养协议，共建博士后工作站，培养企业所需的科研人员和复合型人才。2016年，永新光学与浙江大学、上海理工大学、复旦大学附属医院、南京医科大学合作承担了国家重大科学仪器开发项目

"高分辨荧光显微成像仪研究及产业化"，这是永新光学在产学研合作中受益最大的项目之一。这款高分辨荧光显微成像仪采用大数值孔径物镜成像、微分干涉技术，以及数字化图像显示等技术，可以实现四维全自动分析测量，可应用于肿瘤学、免疫学和细胞生物学领域，具有良好的市场前景，也为永新光学进入显微镜高端市场打下了坚实的基础。

产学研合作使得永新光学产品的技术领先性和质量可靠性大幅提升，在国内的认可度提高后，永新光学有了更强的底气去面对国际厂商。

### 3. 持续创新

2018年，永新光学成功在上海证券交易所上市。上市后，永新光学将更多的资金投入产品研发。2019年，永新光学与浙江大学联合申报的"超分辨光学微纳显微成像技术"项目荣获国家技术发明二等奖。这项技术突破了光学衍射极限，解决了国外超分辨光学成像受到特殊染料限制、适应范围窄的难题，为脑神经、生命科学、纳米制药等领域提供了有力的技术支撑。2019年，永新光学与浙江大学宁波"五位一体"校区教育发展中心、浙江大学光电学院合作，共建浙江大学宁波研究院光电分院，打造出以永新光学为主体，以行业先进技术为引领，汇聚高校和研究院研发能力的深度产学研合作模式，为永新光学在国家重大科研项目中承担重任打下了坚实的基础。

拍下2019年嫦娥四号降落月球第一幕画面的降落相机镜头来自永新光学。这支镜头不仅能帮助嫦娥四号拍下月球崎岖的表面，还能帮助嫦娥四号在降落时避开危险地带，选择安全的地方降落。为了这支镜头，永新光学研发团队兢兢业业，试错很多次，积累了上万套资料和数据。

永新光学依托科技部重点科研专项项目"自动扫描分析系统开发"，在大视野高分辨显微图像、高通量计算机辅助快速检测方面进行攻关，进一步拓展嵌入式显微镜系统业务，向生命科学、生物医学领域进军，相继推出纤维分析仪、血细胞形态分析仪等产品。2021年4月29日，中国空间站"天和"核心舱搭乘长征五号B遥二运载火箭从海南文昌航天发射场成功发射，永新光学研制的中国首台太空荧光显微实验装置也一起出征中国空间站，为航天员进行航天医学、空间生命科学与生物技术研究服务。

从2010年永新光学为嫦娥二号装上"千里眼"，到2020年承制中国首台太空荧光显微实验装置，永新光学持续参与到中国的航空航天事业中。为此，永新光学把"成为值得信赖与尊重的全球知名企业，树立中国科学仪器产品在世界上的优质形象"作为企业愿景，把"为人类认知世界不断提供有效的光学解决方案，实现客户、员工、股东和社会多方价值的持续提升"作为企业使命。

## 【案例来源】

彭新敏，王昕冉，慈建栋.永新光学：阶梯式学习铺就冠军之路［J］.清华管理评论，2021（6）：98-104.

彭新敏，马帅.国际领先客户、国内产学研与后发企业追赶［J］.科学学研究，2023，41（4）：659-668.

## 【案例问题】

1. 永新光学的企业文化是如何形成的？
2. 永新光学"至诚至善、求是创新"的核心价值观是如何影响管理层决策的？

## 【分析提示】

【企业文化、企业强文化】

1. 永新光学企业文化的形成受到企业创始人及管理者一系列决策与行动的影响，企业文化的初始来源反映了企业创立者的愿景，企业文化通过员工选择行为、高层管理者的行动和社会化过程得以维持和延续。可结合上述知识点对永新光学的案例进行分析。

2. 在具有强文化的组织中，员工更加忠诚，绩效也更高。企业文化越强，其对管理者计划、组织、领导和控制方式的影响就越大。可结合上述知识点分析永新光学核心价值观对高层管理者决策及行动的影响。

# 案例 3

## 数益工联助力制造业数字化转型

## 【案例正文】

数益工联是一家致力于打造基于"数据流 + 价值流"的离散制造业数字化软件的公司。数益工联应用新一代的物联网技术与丰富的现场交互手段，融合工业工程精益思想，为离散制造业客户的数字化升级提供从规划到实施落地的端到端工厂级解决方案，专注于打造行业的工业数据平台，持续为客户提供数据智能服务。

数益工联成立于 2020 年 6 月，企业年轻并充满朝气，就是这样一家新兴企业，却已经获得华创资本、高瓴创投和元生资本等知名风投的青睐。2022 年，数益工联的员工已超百人，公司估值已超 5 亿元。

### 1. 工业互联网，"浪潮涌动"

2012 年，美国通用（GE）公司突破性地提出了"工业互联网"这一概念，2013 年，GE 推出以 PaaS（平台即服务）为核心的 Predix 工业云平台，拉开了国际工业互联网云平台发展的序幕。2014 年，GE 联合 AT&T、Cisco、IBM、Intel 等企业成立工业互联网联盟，初步形成行业生态。自此，美国更加注重以创新为驱动，发挥互联网、信息通信、软件等方面的优势，利用信息技术"自上而下"地重塑制造业。

为应对新一轮科技和产业革命带来的挑战，德国更加注重发挥自身在制造装备、自动化系统、工艺流程等方面的优势，利用互联网等信息技术"自下而上"地改造制造业，提出工业 4.0 战略，其本质也是通过连接打通由生产机器构成的"真实"世界和由互联网构成的"虚拟"世界，基于工业互联网重塑新型生产制造服务体系，提高资源配置效率。英国、法国也分别制定了新的工业战略，紧跟全球工业互联网发展动向，加大了对本国工业互联网技术突破、产业布局、金融服务等方面的支持力度。日本提出了"互联工业"战略，试图将人、设备、系统、技术等连接起来，以创造新的附加值和解决相关的社会问题。韩国将人工智能、自动驾驶和 3D 打印确立为智能制造产业发展的主攻方向。

视野转向国内，2015 年我国国务院印发《中国制造 2025》，首次提出制造强国战略。随后工业互联网企业相继诞生，如树根互联等。2019 年，工信部印发《"5G+工业互联网" 512 工程推进方案》，推动工业互联网发展进一步升级。近年来，我国工业互联网产业发展成果显著。在体量方面，2022 年，由工信部指导成立的工业互联网产业联盟的会员数量已超过 2000 家。在服务和产品方面，已经初步形成了核心层、应用层同步发展的系统化平台服务体系，其中核心层平台市场集中度高，垄断格局显著；应用层平台市场集中度低，具有"百花齐放"的特点。

**2. 数益工联，"勇立潮头"**

自工业互联网概念提出以来，国内互联网企业、制造业企业纷纷出手尝试，期望能在工业互联网的领域占据一席之地。例如，华为、阿里巴巴等企业构建了通用的基础性平台和云服务平台，海尔建立了 COSMO 平台来针对传统制造业转型升级的需求，金蝶、浪潮等企业通过轻量级工业 App 帮助中小企业进行基础性的数字化、信息化和自动化改造，徐工、树根互联等企业面向工业互联网平台提供运营服务。虽然众多知名企业的进入使某些核心技术得到突破，但真正能代表工业互联网的 SaaS（软件即服务）技术还需要进一步发展。

2020 年，时任爱柯迪股份有限公司（以下简称爱柯迪）副总经理的何盛华已从清华大学毕业 10 多年，在制造行业工作多年的经验赋予了他对工业互联网前景的敏锐洞察力。在爱柯迪任职期间，何盛华就已经开始着手爱柯迪的工业互联网转型，使 7 个工厂、30 个车间、2300 台生产设备全部完成与数字化的高度融合，从而大幅提高了产品质量、降低了成本、缩短了交货期，将爱柯迪的数字化工厂设想变成了现实。爱柯迪的转型经验让何盛华对工业互联网的理解更加深入，何盛华开始思考："为什么不做一个数字化转型平台，将资源和经验共享呢？"

2020 年 8 月，何盛华毅然辞职并创立了数益工联。何盛华和他的团队不再局限于单一企业的数字化转型，而是运用自己的思想与技术去完成前人未曾实现的 SaaS 层面的产品开发，致力于研发全世界第一个高度标准化的工业互联网平台。SaaS 提供商将为企业搭建信息化所需要的所有网络基础设施及软件、硬件运作平台，并负责前期实施、后期维护等一系列服务，企业无须购买软件和硬件、建设机房、招聘IT人员，就可通过互联网使用信息系统。就像只要打开自来水龙头就能用水一样，企业只需根据实际需要，向SaaS提供商租赁软件服务。

数益工联成立后，何盛华带领他的团队仅仅用了两年的时间，就将SaaS标准化程度提高到跨行业80%标准化、同行业90%标准化的水平，并正在向更高的标准化目标迈进。但这一过程仍然面临很多困难：第一，要明确未来研发过程中哪些功能和标准是可以实现的，哪些非标准化需求需要剔除，这是一个探索的过程；第二，数益工联毕竟不是腾讯、阿里巴巴这样的大企业，没有强大的底蕴做支撑，因此必须加强软件技术方面的投入与研发。

**3. 携手制造业，"继往开来"**

近年来，工业互联网、"未来工厂"所引导的产业数字化和智能化，成为许多制造业企业未来变革的方向。工厂数字化是全球同步的新赛道，这对中国制造业来说，既是挑战也是难得的机遇。何盛华表示，我国有很多制造业企业在全球细分市场上占有率第一，尤其是长三角和珠三角地区的企业，它们购买全球最先进的装备，使用数字化软件实行高度自动化生产，生产了大量的产品。这些先进的制造业企业在中国大量涌现，为数益工联的数字化工厂项目提供了最全的类型和最新的落地现场。

2021年8月，数益工联与美硕电气签订的数字化工厂一期项目圆满落地。此项目涵盖质量管理、异常管理、设备管理、条码管理、人员管理、仓储物流管理、计划报工管理、工艺管理、无纸化文档管理、报表管理共10个模块30项功能，数益工联仅耗时3个月便完成了数字化工厂的实施部署与交付验收。

2021年9月，数益工联与宁波力劲科技签署战略合作协议，双方就宁波力劲科技数字化工厂一期项目达成深度战略合作，选定数控机床车间为实施范围，数益工联仅用3个月就实现了该车间的数字化标杆改造。

2022年3月，宁波力劲科技的数字化工厂二期项目启动，该项目基于一期项目功能模块，新增了多个全新模块，实现了"采购—原材料入库—钣金—数控机床—配件—装配—成品发货—客户使用"全流程的数据打通。

2022年4月，数益工联与海威股份合作的数字化工厂项目正式启动，双方共同打造生产制造过程全透明的全球领先的压铸行业标杆数字化工厂。海威股份期望通过数字化转型升级来提升企业综合竞争力，充分发挥智造引领力，推动最新数字科技与先进制造技术的深度融合，从而让自己快速成为世界级的汽车零部件行业的首选供应商。

数益工联一方面将继续对目前已有的底座产品进行打磨迭代，计划推出100%标准化的SaaS产品；另一方面将扩展产品线，进一步开发年销售额为1000万元以上的中小型制造业客户。

何盛华和他的团队正带领着"年轻"的数益工联，基于深刻的产业经验，发挥物联网、人机交互等技术优势，为离散制造业客户打造标准化、高适配、全链条的工厂数字化解决方案。同时，数益工联也正在以自己的方式，助力我国制造业持续降本增效，为我国提升制造业数字化水平，实现高质量发展，迈向制造强国贡献力量。

## 【案例问题】

1. 数益工联管理层必须面对的外部趋势是什么？这些趋势会如何影响公司管理层的决策？

2. 哪些企业是数益工联重要的利益相关者？这些利益相关者可能具有哪些利益？为什么利益相关者关系管理非常重要？

## 【分析提示】

1. 本案例需要从宏观经济环境和中观行业环境的角度展开分析，可能涉及的知识点有政治、经济、社会、人口、技术、全球化等宏观因素，以及供应方、购买方、替代品、潜在行业进入者、行业内部竞争等行业因素。

2. 本案例需要从利益相关者关系管理角度展开分析。利益相关者包括员工、消费者、股东、供应方、竞争者、社区、政府等。利益相关者的核心利益各不相同，并有可能相互冲突。利益相关者关系管理能为企业带来的好处有：更好地预测外部环境变化，更加成功地创新，增强与利益相关者之间的信任度，更加灵活地应对外部环境变化等。

【环境如何影响管理者？】

## 案例 4

# 青山的绿色管理

## 【案例正文】

青山控股集团有限公司（以下简称青山），是一家专注于不锈钢生产制造的大型重工业企业，公司自创立之初就十分重视环保问题。"绿水青山就是金山银山"，是带领青山从无到有、走向世界的创始人项光达时常挂在嘴边的话语。如果说厂房和装备是企业的躯体，领导者是企业的大脑，那么企业文化就是企业的灵魂，在项光达的言传身教之下，绿色可持续发展理念已经深深嵌入青山的企业文化，被所有青山人铭记于心并付诸实践。多年来，青山人把根植在心中的绿色可持续发展理念认真贯彻到每一个项目的建设和工厂的每一项日常经营管理中。青山坚持高标准、严要求，在不断创新技术与工艺的同时，认真履行自己的环保责任。

### 1. 创新冶炼技术：引入 RKEF 工艺，创新"双联法"

2007 年 3 月，项光达赴印度尼西亚与 Aneka Tambang 公司商谈购买镍矿事宜，并在之后的交流过程中首次接触到 RKEF 工艺。RKEF 工艺是一种高效结合回转窑与热矿炉，利用红土镍矿冶炼精制镍铁的生产工艺，在国外已有几十年的历史，但当时中国却没有一家民营企业采用这种先进的工艺，大部分民营企业采用的依旧是耗能极高的传统 BF 工艺。

为了成功引进国外的 RKEF 工艺，青山请来了当时国内最负盛名的中国恩菲工程技术有限公司做设计规划，并远赴海外向知名钢铁企业取经。2009 年，青山在福安湾坞半岛投资建设 RKEF 镍铁生产线，仅仅经过 18 个月，国内第一条具有自主知识产权的 RKEF 镍铁生产线就成功建成投产，并得以迅速复制和推广，该生产线在提高生产效率的同时，实现了清洁环保和节能降耗的目标。

在创新和绿色可持续发展理念的驱动下，青山率先创造了"RKEF+AOD"工艺，实现了跨领域技术创新，使镍水在不冷却的情况下，直接热送至 AOD 炉，大大降低了热能损耗和生产成本。与传统的生产工艺相比，"RKEF+AOD"工艺可使青山每年节约 72 亿度电，相当于 4 个 100 万人口城市一年的生活用电总量，同时每年可减少排放碳粉尘 200 万吨、二氧化碳 720 万吨、二氧化硫 22 万吨、氮氧化物 11 万吨。

创新是青山快速发展的命脉，永续经营是青山的坚定追求，在首创了"RKEF+AOD"工艺后，青山又踏上了硫化镍矿和 RKEF 工艺的"双联"技术应用创新之路。2014 年，青山投资 2000 万元的硫酸厂建成并试生产，实现了先将硫化镍处理后再应用 RKEF 工艺的创新，这一创新不仅提高了产量，还大大降低了能源消耗量，实现了排放无害化处理。具体来说，生产过程中的尾气可以充分回收并在稀释后得到硫酸以用于后续生产，排放出的粉尘经充分回收后可以加入 RKEF 炉中用于制备粗镍合金，这种循环利用的方式极大地减少了资源的浪费。同时，硫化镍矿在焙烧的过程中会释放出大量的热能，青山将其转化为机械能或电能，极大地降低了企业的能源消耗量，使青山在绿色可持续发展的道路上又迈进了一大步。通过工艺创新，加大资金、技术投入和改善管理，青山努力兑现着自己对环境的承诺。

**2. 节能减排：利用余热发电，巧用皮带运输**

青山正努力加快由资源消耗型企业向资源节约型、环境友好型企业转变的步伐，降低能源消耗、减少废物排放一直是青山努力的方向。

2011 年，青山与上海一家能源公司结缘，并首次接触到大型工业余热余压回收利用技术。经过深入的了解，青山发现余热发电技术能够变废为宝，若能合理利用，这将会是最有效的余热利用途径。

经过一年多的改造与建设，2013 年青山引入项目装机容量达 15 兆瓦的余热发电设备，将生产过程中的烟气余热通过余热锅炉吸收、加热后变成机械能，再通过发电机转化为电能，该余热发电设备全年可发电 1 亿度。

此后，青山不断扩大余热发电技术的应用范围，2016 年共建设了 4 个余热发电项目。2018 年，青山的炼钢 AOD 炉全部由水冷烟罩技术升级为汽化烟罩技术，进一步提高了能源转换再利用效率。

除了引入余热发电技术，青山还开拓了矿区就地建厂的新模式。在印度尼西亚，青山围绕矿区建设厂房，使曾经的荒郊野岭变成如今整洁漂亮、热闹繁忙的工业园。这种模式实现了零距离运输，每年在运输上就能节约 1 万吨标准煤。

此外，青山投资几十亿元兴建红土镍矿皮带运输机、脱硫塔、废水处理等设施，在生产经营的同时，最大限度地实现节能减排。青山斥 2 亿巨资在福建、广东等地建造红土镍矿皮带运输机。红土镍矿从码头、工厂到车间的运输均采用 7.5 千米皮带通廊运输，彻底解决了红土镍矿在汽车运输过程中"跑冒滴漏"的问题。这种封闭式运输还避免了汽车运输的扬尘污染，确保了厂区和周边环境的清洁。青山还建立并完善了能源消耗和废物排放在线监测系统。青山一直严格要求自己，例如，其工厂排放的烟气中的硫含量远远低于国家制定的排放标准。

### 3. 资源再利用：研制塑料粒子，回收废不锈钢

青山在生产过程中始终坚持经济循环的理念，对生产环节中的废气、废水和固体废物都会进行最大限度的循环利用。

在实际使用"RKEF+ 硫化镍矿"双联法进行生产的过程中，为了对镍精矿进行打包，硫酸厂会购买一定数量的包装袋，但如何处理使用过的废旧包装袋是一件非常令人头疼的事情。废旧包装袋上通常会残留很多镍精矿，直接清洗袋子会造成重金属污染，这就会违背青山对于环保的承诺。

为了解决这一难题，青山考察了多种实施方案，最终确定了把废旧包装袋压缩成颗粒的方法。2016 年，青山硫酸厂的塑料粒子项目正式启动，该项目的厂房为 900 平方米，于 10 月建成投产。塑料粒子项目的运行并不是一帆风顺的，如项目流程工艺、厂房选址等问题都曾阻碍青山前进的步伐，但主动承担社会环保责任的理念不断激励着青山克服了一个又一个困难。青山在环保方面始终是不遗余力的，它在建成塑料粒子制造厂的同时，又引入了水循环系统，避免了污水的排放。

硫酸厂的塑料粒子项目，不仅取得了良好的市场效益，还达到了最为重要的资源回收利用这一目的。清洗过废旧包装的每升水中含有 2500～3500 毫克镍矿，把水浇筑到镍金砂中，在镍金砂经过蒸发后对其进行冶炼，最终又能冶炼成不锈钢。如果废旧包装处理不当，会造成严重的环境污染问题，但在采用了**塑料粒子方法后**，青山实现了镍矿和水资源的全部回收利用，真正做到了零排放，保护了生态环境。

青山已成立 30 多年，作为世界领先的不锈钢制造企业，青山始终将绿色管理和

可持续发展放在企业发展的核心位置。多年来，青山创新冶炼技术，降低能耗，重视节能减排，将资源回收再利用落到实处，不断通过实际行动向世人表明青山对绿色可持续发展理念的坚持。一直以来，青山没有一味地追求经济利润，而是积极承担起社会责任，确保企业环保达标，既要"金山银山"，更要"绿水青山"！

### 【案例问题】

1. 结合案例阐述什么是绿色管理，以及青山是如何进行绿色管理的？
2. 青山践行绿色可持续发展理念的行为有哪些？这些行为对青山有哪些回馈？

### 【分析提示】

1. 本案例需要从企业绿色管理、绿色行动，以及企业文化、使命、愿景、核心价值观等方面来分析青山在绿色管理方面的所作所为以及其进行绿色管理的意义。

【企业是否应该承担社会责任？】

2. 从企业可持续发展的角度，对青山所涉及的各个方面的环保行为进行分析，总结青山有哪些可持续发展行为，以及这些行为在经济效益和非经济效益方面分别给青山带来了什么样的影响。

# 案例 5

## 天港公益基金的"橙计划"

## 【案例正文】

2011年8月，宁波本土企业天港酒店的创始人龚浩强带领天港酒店员工成立了天港公益基金。自此，天港公益基金"橙计划"志愿服务项目正式启动，天港酒店主动承担起关爱留守儿童、为他们带去温暖的责任。"橙计划"取意冰心笔下的《小橘灯》，旨在用一抹温暖的橙色照亮希望，为孩子打开一扇通往外部世界的大门，为孩子点亮一条不一样的成长之路。"橙计划"的帮扶对象被称为"橙长之星"，志愿者则被称为"橙子"。截至2021年，"橙计划"汇聚各类志愿者200余人，累计服务留守儿童3525人次，服务时间超过4万小时，帮扶范围覆盖吉林、云南、贵州、黑龙江、广西、湖南等14个省份的140多个县市。10多年来，"橙计划"项目不曾间断，随着时间的打磨越来越完善。

### 1. 形成三大核心项目的全面扶助

2013年7月，天港公益基金聚焦服务行业从业人员家中的留守儿童，形成了以"助学、成长辅导、快乐体验营"三大项目为核心的"橙计划"慈善活动体系。项目主要面向小学一年级到高中三年级学龄段的孩子，对成为"橙长之星"的孩子开展以"助学、成长辅导、快乐体验营"为主的全面扶助，让孩子成为直接受益者，快乐成长。

助学：每年针对每位"橙长之星"进行物资帮扶。不仅以助学金的形式帮助孩子们渡过求学的难关，还贴心地为孩子们准备了心愿卡，帮助他们实现心愿。

成长辅导：帮助"橙长之星"与其父母进行情感交流以及沟通。"橙子"通过与"橙长之星"一对一结对，对孩子进行情感引导，帮孩子建立良好、健康的心理环境；同时通过留守儿童家长咨询热线，指导父母应如何与远方的孩子进行沟通，从而在孩子与父母之间搭建沟通的桥梁。除此之外，"橙计划"还充分运用政府、企业、专业机构等社会公益力量建立的家长学校，打通孩子与父母的双向"成长辅导"之路；开设家长学校线上线下课堂，打破传统课堂在时间与空间上的限制，通过远程互动，扩大受众群体。

快乐体验营：每年暑假举办面向"橙长之星"的夏令营活动，每年邀请30～50名"橙长之星"来宁波与父母团聚，参加为期7天的夏令营。夏令营根据年度主题及孩子的年龄段特点，设计不同的课程体验内容，包括传统文化教育、心理和生理健康教育、安全教育、角色体验、军训、自然宁波、人文宁波、阳明国学堂、爱国主义教育等，让孩子们通过视觉、听觉、触觉以及味觉全方位地感受宁波，通过"与爸爸妈妈一起上班"的职业体验感受父母的辛劳，从而增进孩子们与父母的感情和相互理解，为孩子们打开一扇通往外部世界的大门。夏令营以"快乐体验"为目的，无论是满足孩子们愿望的"心愿时间"还是团队拓展互动游戏，都力求带给孩子们一段难忘的快乐之旅。

除了三大核心帮扶项目，天港公益基金还积极参与公益发声活动，呼吁社会公众给予留守儿童关爱。天港公益基金还设置专款用于资助有关留守儿童的调研及图书出版，已资助出版《在一起——中国留守儿童报告》等作品。天港公益基金定期举办公益论坛、慈善晚宴等活动，以吸引更多的社会关注，鼓励更多人探讨并参与到关爱留守儿童的事业中来。另外，天港公益基金还拍摄留守儿童纪录片，关心青少年心理健康、安全及教育问题。

**2. 志愿者队伍不断壮大**

2014年8月，为了更好地服务慈善活动，天港公益基金成立了"橙子俱乐部"，建立起志愿者管理培训体系。这不但为"橙计划"设立了完整的志愿者招募、培训、管理体系，建立了"橙子"选拔与专业培训体系，还逐步将志愿者队伍从宁波扩展至留守儿童所在地，打破了远距离沟通的限制。

自"橙计划"启动以来，"橙子"的队伍不断壮大。目前，"橙计划"的志愿者不仅包括来自天港公益基金的志愿者，还包括热爱志愿活动、乐于助人、关爱他人的大学生志愿者和社会志愿者。"橙子"包括：义工志愿者——在项目活动期间提供短期服务支持；结对志愿者——长期对孩子进行一对一的成长辅导及帮扶；资源志愿者——提供资源支持，如媒体资源、教研资源；明星志愿者——各领域专家或关键意见领袖，为项目发声呼吁。

2018年4月，天港公益基金在黔西南州成立"橙计划"第一支当地志愿者队伍。2020年8月，天港公益基金在延边州落地"橙计划"项目，并成立第二支当地志愿者队伍。天港公益基金还在积极建立更多的当地志愿者队伍，寻求在更多的地区落地"橙计划"项目。

**3. "橙计划"走入四川凉山州**

2021年，宁波与四川凉山州形成帮扶结对合作。天港公益基金作为中华少年儿童慈善救助基金会的一员，积极响应号召，邀请品学兼优、家境贫困的四川凉山州的孩子加入天港公益基金"橙计划"的帮扶结对项目，成为"橙长之星"。

天港公益基金"橙计划"项目组通过入户走访，了解了部分学生的家庭生活状况，对这些学生表达了亲切的关怀和慰问，并送上千元奖学金和"橙计划"快乐体验营邀请函。帮扶结对项目依托"橙计划"完整的公益生态链，为凉山州的"橙长之星"们改善物质生活环境、家庭环境以及社会舆论环境，帮助孩子们塑造自信、自立、自强的健康人格。

此外，"橙计划"项目落地凉山州之后，通过凉山州的志愿者支队，把项目资源引入当地，把关爱工作本地化、日常化，不断扩大"橙计划"对社会影响的外延效益，把宁波的物质资源和精神帮扶注入凉山州的每一个"橙长之星"的家庭，真正让关爱留守儿童的"宁波模式"走进凉山州。

2011年至今，天港启动"橙计划"已经十多年了。基于多年积累的"橙计划"慈善活动经验，天港公益基金打造了一条完整的关爱留守儿童的公益生态链。该生态链覆盖留守儿童、留守儿童家长、公益志愿者、社会公众等各类相关群体，为"如何帮助留守儿童"这一社会问题提供了一个模板，被政府部门评价为关爱留守儿童的"宁波模式""宁波方法"。2016年9月，天港公益基金"橙计划"案例在全国302个优秀年度品牌营销案例中脱颖而出，荣获第十五届中国杰出品牌营销奖。"橙计划"为留守儿童带去了温暖、快乐和希望，天港公益基金也为解决留守儿童这一社会性问题贡献出了自己的一份力量。

## 【案例问题】

1. 天港公益基金的"橙计划"属于社会义务、社会响应还是社会责任?
2. 从管理者的角度阐释"橙计划"为天港酒店带来了哪些益处。

## 【分析提示】

1. 本案例围绕天港公益基金的慈善事业展开,从慈善事业的发起、发展、成就以及意义等方面进行了描述,展现了天港公益基金"橙计划"的历史、变化以及取得的效果,主要涉及的知识点包括社会义务、社会响应和社会责任等概念,以及影响企业社会责任方面的决策的因素。

【社会义务?
社会响应?
社会责任?】

2. 从管理者的角度,对天港公益基金"橙计划"所涉及的组织道德行为进行分析,总结天港酒店组织道德所经历的几个时期,以及每个时期的特点,同时结合天港酒店的战略、使命、愿景和组织文化,分析组织道德和企业社会责任为企业带来的益处。

## 案例 6

# 缸鸭狗的传承与创新

# 【案例正文】

缸鸭狗是一家以销售汤圆为主的食品品牌。"三更四更半夜头，要吃汤团缸鸭狗。一碗下肚勿肯走，两碗三碗发瘾头。"这句在宁波口耳相传的俗语体现了老宁波人对缸鸭狗汤圆的肯定。

1926年，宁波人江定法在城隍庙摆摊卖汤圆，并在不久后以自己的小名"江阿狗"的谐音"缸鸭狗"作为店名，在开明街设立店铺，一个水缸、一只草鸭、一只黄狗的鲜活招牌形象就由此诞生了。1993年，缸鸭狗被商务部授予"中华老字号"企业称号。1997年，缸鸭狗汤圆被中国烹饪协会评为"中华名小吃"。

改革开放后，随着国外快餐品牌进入中国，老字号品牌"缸鸭狗"的荣光逐渐黯淡。2007年，由于旧城改造，缸鸭狗告别了坚守10年的城隍庙美食街旺铺，一夜之间经营面积从1200平方米缩减至100平方米，缸鸭狗也面临着被收购易主的窘境。宁波本地人陈开河怀着对传统品牌缸鸭狗的喜爱和振兴品牌的雄心，努力协调各方关系，说服了缸鸭狗当时的老股东，最终买下缸鸭狗的所有股权。2009年，陈开河成为缸鸭狗新一代掌门人。

## 1. 缸鸭狗品牌复活

陈开河接手后的缸鸭狗面临诸多问题，其中经营成本增加、品质下滑、利润变薄等问题尤为突出。缸鸭狗亟待转变消费者眼中"没落老字号"的刻板印象，实现品牌复活。陈开河决定对缸鸭狗实施以下变革：第一，发扬品牌的优秀传统，重视汤圆品质；第二，重构供应链体系，拓宽营销渠道；第三，调查市场需求，并以此为依据调整营销策略以及产品品类。

陈开河认为，缸鸭狗汤圆之所以深受老宁波人的喜爱，不仅是因为其拥有悠久的历史和团圆的寓意，更是因为缸鸭狗严格遵循选材、浸泡、磨浆、压榨、制馅、包制这六道传统工艺。黑芝麻猪油汤圆一直是缸鸭狗最著名的产品，黑芝麻油性充盈，甜而不腻，当年，老一代掌门人江定法对汤圆原料的选择极其考究，其中的米粉是用本地产的上等白糯米研磨而成的，猪油用的是优质有厚度的肉猪板油。此外，缸鸭狗传统上一直采用水磨工艺，即先将糯米从固体变成液体，再通过压制蒸熟将液体重新凝固。水磨工艺不但能使糯米的口感发挥到最佳，而且保证了汤圆皮的嫩滑。但是手工制作汤圆的工序已经非常复杂了，如果连糯米都要现磨，那么成本会大大增加，仅一个污水处理系统就需要上百万元。陈开河思虑再三，还是决定保留水磨工艺。他认为，水磨工艺是缸鸭狗保持其独特性的关键环节，只有把所有的工艺做到极致，产品才会物有所值。

为了提高汤圆品质，缸鸭狗必须在继承、延续的基础上发扬创新精神。陈开河在镇海区九龙湖建立高标准食品工厂，并成立了"健康食品与生物技术研究所"，购置了大量的现代化机械设备，将制作流程标准化。

提高品质是品牌复活的重要环节，但如今已经不是酒香不怕巷子深的时代了，打造一条高效合理的营销通路很重要。陈开河一直在思考：究竟应该如何让缸鸭狗这碗宁波汤圆走出浙江，呈现在全国人民的餐桌上？仅靠线下门店销售还远远不够，应当推出速冻汤圆，将营销渠道拓展至大型商超。

通过市场调研，陈开河发现，我国速冻食品市场以水饺、汤圆为主。据统计，2020年，在速冻食品业中，三全、思念、龙凤、湾仔码头四个品牌的市场占有率达70%。其中三全的市场占有率达到27%，后三者的市场占有率分别为20%、12%和11%。早期，缸鸭狗也曾研发过速冻汤圆，但由于产品过于单一，整体竞争力远不如多元化、系列化的三全、思念、龙凤等国内知名的速冻食品品牌，再加上三雪等当地品牌的迅速崛起不断弱化着缸鸭狗的市场地位及其在市民心中的传统记忆，缸鸭狗速冻汤圆没过多长时间就被挤出了市场。速冻汤圆行业的竞争愈加激烈，对于缸鸭狗来说选择合适的商业模式拓展市场至关重要。

市面上最畅销的三全、思念等品牌的汤圆售价较便宜，缸鸭狗如果与其拼价格、拼产量显然是行不通的。陈开河认为，改革开放后，国民消费水平得到空前提高，高品质的产品更能吸引顾客。缸鸭狗定位为中国最高端的汤圆，价格必须与品质匹配，只要贵得有理由，销路就不用发愁。因此，在消费者识别方面，缸鸭狗将目标消费者锁定为中高收入群体。不同于市面上的速冻汤圆，缸鸭狗主打中高端市场，汤圆均价也较同类产品高出一倍。2015年春节期间，缸鸭狗入驻四季联华超市，在元宵节还未到时，缸鸭狗的汤圆就已经卖断货了。品质与品牌、独特的匠心与深厚的文化，支撑起缸鸭狗汤圆远高于同类品牌汤圆的定价。

解决了速冻汤圆的定位问题，接下来如何将汤圆销往全国市场也是令陈开河颇为苦恼的问题。调制好的汤圆常常会出现塌架、有明显裂纹、脱粉、包馅开裂等现象，影响了质量和美观。为此，重新构建一条缸鸭狗专属的特色供应链，对保证缸鸭狗汤圆的品质来说尤为重要。陈开河发现，行业内速冻汤圆的生产商大多是和一些物流公司签订协议，由这些物流公司采用冷链运输方式将汤圆从食品工厂运送到各大商场，但在这种运输方式下，仍然无法避免出现汤圆在运输途中被震碎的情况。相比之下，国际知名冰激凌品牌哈根达斯的冷链运输模式，是从出厂到销售终端都采用恒温的冷链，由中央厨房统一配送至各餐饮店，更加安全高效。因此，陈开河决定参考哈根达斯的做法，建立自己的冷链运输系统。

除了将速冻汤圆引入大型商超，陈开河在销售渠道方面也进行了适应性调整。缸鸭狗以大型商超为主，同时兼顾连锁餐饮通路，在自己开设餐饮门店的同时，与众多知名餐饮品牌，如海底捞、理象国、喜茶等合作，并向希尔顿、开元、康得思等高端酒店提供缸鸭狗汤圆的直送服务。

**2. 缸鸭狗的数字化转型**

随着电子商务在中国的蓬勃发展，众多企业开始迈入数字化时代。淘宝、京东、盒马等线上平台以其强大的引流能力、方便快捷的购物体验，对传统线下商超形成降维打击，缸鸭狗所处的食品行业也面临着数字化转型的冲击。

陈开河决定实施数字化转型，并为缸鸭狗数字化转型制定了四步走的发展战略：第一步，入驻线上平台，实现数字化接入，借力大型销售平台，实现销售增长以及相关数据收集；第二步，开展数字化营销，通过小红书等引流渠道，增加名气，吸引消费者；第三步，开展数字化产品研发，通过大数据，了解市场青睐的食品种类，在主营商品汤圆中融入相关元素，让汤圆更具时代气息；第四步，打造企业运营数字化底座，将缸鸭狗的生产、销售、财务、管理整合到一个平台上，推动经营管理数字化。

2016 年，缸鸭狗入驻淘宝等电商平台，拓展线上销售渠道；同年，缸鸭狗与盒马合作，找寻打入全国市场的通路。不同于传统商超，盒马作为新零售平台，其采用的数字化管理方式，可以将更多营运数据和预测反馈给企业，为企业进行产品创新提供数据支持。基于盒马的大数据和用户调研，陈开河发现，传统规格汤圆一包 16 颗，多数消费者一餐根本无法吃完，容易造成浪费，而小规格、有卖点、方便吃的食品更受青睐。于是，陈开河决定适应性地调整产品，调整汤圆规格，推出专供盒马的小包装汤圆。2018 年，缸鸭狗在盒马的销售额比上年增加了约 15 倍。

数据是陈开河作出有效决策的重要工具。缸鸭狗借助抖音、小红书、微博等平台，一方面进行引流，另一方面不断对消费者进行精准画像，分析消费者偏好和需求。针对目标群体年轻化的特征，缸鸭狗推出榴莲、抹茶、高粱奶黄、玫瑰等口味的速冻汤圆，以及手工酒酿、糖桂花、即食包子等特色单品。陈开河注意到，平时忙于学业、工作的年轻人，是老字号品牌较难触及的消费群体，因为相比于堂食，这部分消费者热衷于订购外卖。缸鸭狗要想辐射这批消费者，布局线上外卖业务势在必行。2020 年，缸鸭狗外卖小程序试运营，首月销售额就达到了 49.3 万元，订单量近 1 万单，不仅得到了喜爱缸鸭狗的老顾客的捧场，也获得了大江南北初识缸鸭狗的新顾客的青睐。

2021 年，缸鸭狗与"微盟"合作，打造"微信小程序外卖平台＋线上商城＋线下实体店"三店一体的营销模式。陈开河力图借助一体化形式的会员生态，对消费者进行价值输出，让年轻消费者认识并关注到缸鸭狗，再逐步从公域外卖平台向私域小程序引流。2021 年，缸鸭狗的微信小程序会员已达到 30 万人，陈开河计划将会员规模扩大至 500 万人。从布局线上数字化销售开始，缸鸭狗的线上销售量不断提高。

此外，陈开河也格外重视经营管理的数字化转型。由于缸鸭狗的管理团队在借助企业微信进行日常办公交流时存在诸多数据传输壁垒，增加了管理成本，因此，缸鸭狗致力于打造企业数字化底座，将缸鸭狗的生产信息、销售信息、财务信息、合作方信息、门店销售情况等都整合在一个系统中，从而提升管理效率，辅助管理层作出科学决策。

经营管理数字化转型将是缸鸭狗未来几年转型的重要内容，它无疑也是老字号品牌持续创新、焕发活力的关键。

## 【案例来源】

张逸龙. 缸鸭狗：变与不变　彰显匠心之道［J］. 宁波通讯，2020（14）：72-75.

黄明朗. "见说'陈家'滴粉好，试灯风里卖元宵"：记缸鸭狗股份有限公司董事长陈开河［J］. 宁波通讯，2019（4）：52-55.

## 【案例问题】

1. 本案例中有哪些关键的决策？它们是如何作出的？
2. 请分析缸鸭狗管理者是如何利用大数据作出决策的。

## 【分析提示】

1. 本案例中的关键决策有传承水磨工艺、研发速冻产品、入驻线上平台、开拓外卖业务、拓展延伸产品等，这一系列决策让老字号品牌缸鸭狗在市场潮流中历久弥新，持续成长。可以结合不同类型的决策和管理者不同的思维模式等相关知识进行分析，如决策可以分为程序化决策和非程序化决策，管理者有线性和非线性两种不同思维模式。管理者的线性思维模式是指偏向使用外部数据，通过理性和逻辑思考处理信息；非线性思维模式是指偏向使用内部信息，使用内在洞察力、感受和直觉处理信息。

【管理决策：理性？有限理性？直觉？】

2. 结合案例中管理者利用线上数据进行产品创新的例子来说明大数据在决策中

的作用，正确认识大数据和决策的关系。大数据是辅助管理者进行决策的强大工具，然而，不论大数据有多么全面或被进行了多么深入的分析，都需要管理者良好的判断力来调和。

# 案例 7

## 宁波慈星的新产品开发

## 【案例正文】

宁波慈星股份有限公司（以下简称慈星）创立于1988年，是中国电脑横机领域的上市企业，是国家级火炬计划项目实施单位，荣获过国家科技进步二等奖等荣誉。2021年，慈星研制的KS系列全成型电脑横机颠覆了传统针织横机的编织工艺，实现了针织毛衫的一次成型编织，代表了当前前沿的电脑横机技术，具有极大的技术创新性。慈星从2010年开始筹划进入全成型电脑横机领域，直到2021年终于研制出了代表行业最高水平的KS系列全成型电脑横机，10年来慈星咬定"目标"不放松，周密计划、精心部署，最终取得了重大技术突破和市场成功。

### 1. 通过跨国并购进入全成型电脑横机领域

随着3D打印、人工智能等技术的兴起，以及受人工成本上涨和缝合工序人手短缺等因素的影响，一些行业领先企业在20世纪末开始研究全成型电脑横机[①]，如1999年日本岛精首次开发了四针板全成型电脑横机并申请了专利，2003年德国斯托尔推出两针板全成型电脑横机。全成型技术不仅能减少缝合的工序从而节省人工成本，而且能大幅度减少废纱从而使生产更节能环保，还能提高衣服的舒适度，因此逐渐成为横机行业新的技术发展方向。但由于全成型电脑横机成本较高，主要面向高端客户，市场需求量较小，因此2018年之前全球市场上的主流机型仍是电脑横机。慈星作为国内电脑横机领域的头部企业，自2010年开始关注全成型技术，当时市场上已存在两针板、四针板、五针板等多种全成型技术设计。

2008年，国际金融危机爆发，全球第三大电脑横机生产商瑞士事坦格因经营困难意欲寻找买家，这给慈星通过海外并购快速提高全成型技术水平带来了难得的机遇。2010年，慈星成功收购事坦格，并接收了其研发团队和先进的嵌花技术。

---

① 从全球范围行业技术演变来看，针织横机经历了手摇横机（1900—1960年）、电脑横机（1960—2000年）和全成型电脑横机（2000年至今）三代不同技术范式的更迭。

并购初期，慈星尚不具有全成型电脑横机的独立研发能力，且当时电脑横机仍是公司最大的主营业务，于是公司高管一致决定让并购后的事坦格独立负责全成型电脑横机的研发，在其原有的四针板和嵌花技术的基础上进行改进，慈星仅负责后续的调试和组装工作。

利用事坦格研发全成型电脑横机对并购初期的慈星来说，是成本最低、收益最高的战略计划，事实也证明该计划取得了良好的成效。2012年，慈星在全成型技术上取得了发明专利，2015年制作出了工程样机，2017年试制了第一台全成型电脑横机Taurus。慈星的Taurus一经展出便被称为毛衫行业的一个里程碑设计，开启了国内针织行业的新方向。

然而，慈星在对全成型电脑横机进行市场推广的过程中却遇到了困难。虽然慈星拥有国内优质的营销渠道和销售网络，并积累了大量的客户和营销知识，但由于Taurus采用的是复合针设计，成本很高，一根针就要100元，是普通针价格的10倍，且换针较为不便，无法满足国内客户对全成型电脑横机的价格定位和操作需求，因此在市场上与日本岛精等公司的全成型电脑横机相比，并不具备竞争力。慈星虽然在全成型电脑横机市场的第一次尝试以失败告终，但也积累了许多关于全成型电脑横机的研发经验。

**2. 通过联合研发取得产品创新成功**

2017年，由于劳动力成本上升和企业转型升级的需要，下游针织企业对自动化程度更高的全成型电脑横机的需求大幅上升，但许多横机生产企业因考虑到全成型电脑横机高昂的价格而不愿投入研发。慈星敏锐地发现了这一市场需求，决定加大力度推进全成型电脑横机的研发，并尽可能降低制造成本。

2018年年初，慈星决定由国内技术部、研发部与事坦格共同研发全成型电脑横机，并采取了两种研发设计并行的计划：一方面，国内技术部、研发部与事坦格合作继续推进四针板复合针的设计；另一方面，国内技术部、研发部独立研发两针板加普通针的新架构。同年，慈星建立全成型研究院，主要负责结构设计、工艺研究和制版系统的开发等。

为加快研发进程，慈星加强了与事坦格的协作。国内外研发团队沟通频繁，国外团队定期向国内技术总监汇报进度，同时国内团队积极邀请事坦格的专家来中国进行机器的试制和调试。在公司内部，各部门协同作战，凝聚各方力量，形成工作闭环。例如，在新机型开发出来后，技术部针对新机型进行打样，测试其功能和稳定性，将测试中发现的问题和改善建议反馈到研发部，研发部进行功能性改进后，技术部再进行印证，通过不断反馈互动改善机器性能。

经过近一年的努力，两针板全成型电脑横机 KS3-72 率先研制成功，这款机型采用了特殊的牵拉部件"针耙"，成功地用普通针替代了复合针，大幅降低了成本。此外，在 Taurus 机型商业化失败后，慈星发现事坦格原有的制版系统不适合中国师傅的习惯，因此联合事坦格重新开发出了 Model 制版软件，改变了软件原有的欧式风格，使其更加适合中国师傅的操作习惯。为了实现全成型电脑横机的大批量生产，2019 年慈星投入建成了全成型电脑横机智能制造车间。慈星两针板全成型电脑横机量产后，凭借其仅为日本岛精同类产品价格三分之一的售价快速在国内市场站稳了脚跟。不过，此时慈星在高端全成型电脑横机领域与日本岛精还存在一定的差距。

### 3. 通过"设计增补"打造新技术优势

为了应对来自慈星的竞争，日本岛精也推出了自己的两针板全成型电脑横机，与慈星展开了直接的技术设计竞争。慈星为了巩固具有自主知识产权的全成型技术，逐渐调整之前的技术策略，采取了"设计增补"的技术策略，即围绕自己的核心技术不断进行后续优化和改进。

"设计增补"的技术策略要求公司不断推出新产品，从而形成技术的主导范式，塑造其他公司难以模仿的技术优势。为了抢占市场先机，慈星制订了奖励制度，对超额或超进度完成指标的部门和员工进行奖励和表彰。

明确的目标、周密的计划，使慈星终于实现了全成型电脑横机的系列化。在架构设计上，慈星一方面在原有 10.2 英寸两针板机型的基础上，陆续开发出 13.2 英寸、4.2 英寸、6.2 英寸等不同规格的机型；另一方面在原来事坦格四针板技术的基础上，将原有的复合针改为普通针，同时改进了牵拉装置，2019 年开发出了业内全新的全成型五针板设计,在达到了十八针针织效果的同时大大降低了设备成本。在元件开发上,慈星主要是把昂贵的复合针替换为普通针,并首创了国内最细针距的十八针技术,这种技术可以实现满针编织,最大限度地实现高密度编织。此外,慈星在 KS3 产品基础上进一步对电动纱嘴的独立控制系统进行了优化,使其能够在水平方向自由移动,让纱嘴能够精准定位和同步喂纱。通过元件的优化升级,慈星全成型电脑横机的品质得到进一步提升,成本得到进一步压缩,产品在市场中更具竞争力。

2019 年和 2020 年,慈星共出售 2600 多台全成型电脑横机,全球市场占有率达到 20%,预计到 2025 年其市场占有率将达到 35%,有望成为全球全成型电脑横机领域的领先企业。

## 【案例问题】

1. 在慈星计划策略方向的改变方面,目标发挥着什么作用?

2. 在全成型电脑横机领域中,企业进行新产品开发时需要制订什么类型的计划方案?

3. 在本案例中,什么因素会影响高层管理者的计划?

4. 在慈星发展成行业领先企业的过程中,慈星高层管理者可能会面临什么样的挑战?他们该如何应对?

## 【分析提示】

【目标设定】

1. 目标能够为管理决策和行动提供方向和指导,并且构成用以测量实际效果的标准。以目标为导向的管理是现在使用最广泛的管理方法之一。大量的实例证明,在企业计划策略方向的改变上,清晰的目标可以发挥激励作用;可以提高管理水平,有助于管理者分清组织任务和结构,根据人们承担工作任务的预期结果进行授权;有助于鼓励员工完成各自的目标和组织目标;有助于建立有效的控制机制,衡量结果并采取纠正偏差的行动。可以结合上述目标管理知识及慈星全成型电脑横机开发过程进行分析。

2.根据计划方案的宽度、时间框架、具体性以及使用频率，可以分别将计划方案分为战略方案和业务方案、短期方案和长期方案、指导性方案和具体方案、一次性方案和持续性方案。可以结合上述分类方法以及全成型电脑横机领域的特点进行分析。

3.制订计划方案的过程会受到三种权变因素的影响，即组织层次，环境的不确定性程度和未来承诺的持续时间。在组织层次方面，高层管理者更多地从宏观的角度思考问题、制订战略计划。在环境的不确定性程度方面，当不确定性程度很高时，高层管理者必须随时准备应对变化或者在方案实施过程中对方案作出修改。在未来承诺的持续时间方面，计划应该扩展到未来足够长远的期限上，期限太长或太短的计划都是缺乏效率和效果的。

4.在企业成为行业领先企业的过程中，外部环境是不断变化的，企业高层管理者可能会遇到原有计划不再奏效的情况。企业高层管理者应该在不确定的环境中制订具体但有弹性的计划，即使在面临非常不确定的环境时，仍须制订正式的计划以评估组织绩效，还要建立更加扁平化的组织层次以帮助企业在动态环境中作出更有效的决策。

# 案例 8

## 海伦钢琴的转型升级

## 【案例正文】

海伦钢琴股份有限公司（以下简称海伦钢琴）成立于2001年，主要经营钢琴制造等业务，是国家火炬计划重点高新技术企业、国家文化出口重点企业，荣获"中国驰名商标"称号。海伦钢琴制造的立式钢琴、三角钢琴在国际上已获广泛认可和好评，产品远销欧洲、美国、日本等地。基于智能钢琴的教育培训是海伦钢琴的新兴业务。2019年，海伦钢琴与中央音乐学院继续教育学院共同开发"中央音乐学院继续教育学院·海伦智能钢琴实验课室"项目，由中央音乐学院的名师研发教材，对海伦钢琴在各地区的授权加盟商的授课教师进行培训与指导，将教学效果与艺术考级并轨，从而更有效地开展钢琴教学工作，开启了艺术教育和钢琴教学的新时代。作为一家民营企业，海伦钢琴完整地经历了从无到有、从生产配件到生产整琴、从制造业到服务业的转型升级。

### 1. 一代奠基：从五金"码克"到整琴制造

在海伦钢琴成立之前，公司创始人陈海伦经营着一家五金配件厂，该厂的主要业务是为国内钢琴公司提供配件。当时的钢琴市场主要由广州、上海、营口、北京四个城市的钢琴公司占领，竞争非常激烈。陈海伦梦想可以带领工厂走上一个新的平台，他将目光瞄向了钢琴的"发动机"——核心零部件"码克"。这意味着海伦钢琴要对主导产品进行一次升级改造，在技术工艺方面做到全国领先，要打造一条优质高档的生产流水线。人才、技术和制造工具是海伦钢琴必须解决的难题。幸运的是，当时北京星海公司和奥地利文德隆公司为其提供了先进的技术支持。另外，陈海伦还从日本引进了先进的五轴联动设备。从2001年开始购买到2002年完成工厂整体升级，只用了一年的时间，海伦钢琴便完成了设备的更新换代。2003年3月，在德国法兰克福的展会上，陈海伦向世界展示了自己的"码克"产品。产品一经展出，便受到了外国厂商的追捧。但也是在这一次的展会上，陈海伦发现当时中国企业的思维还普遍停留在节省成本，保证产品一时的质量上，而外国厂商会考虑到产品几十年后的变化,并为此投入人力和财力。这种理念的差异让陈海伦深刻意识到了技术和人才的重要性。此后,陈海伦花重金聘请专家来厂指导,甚至将当时年利润的一半拿来支付人才佣金。

从配件"码克"转向整琴制造是海伦钢琴进行的一次变革。为避免与国内老牌厂商竞争,失去资金来源,陈海伦采取了用配件养钢琴的策略,同时海伦钢琴生产的钢琴全部销往欧洲,不流入国内市场。2004年,海伦钢琴生产的500架钢琴全部被欧洲市场所接受。由此陈海伦知道自己成功了,于是开始放弃五金配套业务。他以自己的名字注册"HAILUN"商标,成立海伦钢琴,并于2005年正式进入国内市场。2019年,海伦钢琴年销售量达10.5万台,位列全球第四。在国内市场上,海伦钢琴的销售量保持着前三的位置。海伦钢琴于2012年在深交所正式上市。海伦钢琴的一代领导人确立的"稳扎稳打"发展理念也深刻影响了继任者的目标塑造,继任者由此开启了新的创业征程。

**2. 父子共事:从整琴制造到智能钢琴开发**

从2012年海伦钢琴上市开始,其对智能钢琴的研发便已提上日程,这一研发历程凝聚着父子两代人的心血。2010年,陈海伦的独子陈朝峰正式进入公司,拥有软件开发经验的他正是开发智能钢琴业务的不二人选。进入公司后,陈朝峰并未急于开展管理工作,而是先在工厂车间轮岗,从而对整琴制作有了初步的了解。之后,他开始负责IPO,并掌管对外投资。这时恰逢公司建设新厂房,陈朝峰又主持了流水线工艺设计。通过总结学习,陈朝峰的个人能力得到了飞速提升。2013年,陈朝峰开始在一代领导人的指导下主持智能钢琴的研发工作。

海伦钢琴虽然在传统钢琴制造方面占据了行业领先地位,但在智能化科技领域还是一个"新兵"。作为一家初创型组织,陈朝峰的团队取得了丰硕的成果,当然也走了不少弯路。在与北京邮电大学的合作失败后,陈朝峰开始组建自己的团队,力求自主研发。在这个过程中,陈海伦给予其充分的支持。一方面,团队借鉴欧美的先进经验,在音频同步、电流杂音等方面进行深入研究。由于一切都是创新尝试,因此芯片功能难免会不稳定,陈朝峰团队根据问题和意见不断修改,使产品逐渐趋于完善。另一方面，团队还在不断完善远程音乐交流功能。由于智能钢琴对音质要求比较特殊，传统网络已不能满足这一要求。海伦钢琴利用5G网络实现了远程音乐的同步传输，远程传输中的音质无损成为海伦智能钢琴的优势。此外，开发自动演奏功能也是团队要攻坚的内容，即当一方在线演奏出一首曲子时，网络另一端的智能钢琴便可重现这首曲子的演奏，在力度、按键序等方面达到统一，便于教师指导学生学习。未来这一功能可用于远程音乐的实时培训。2014年，为了配合智能钢琴项目的研发，海伦钢琴成立了全资子公司"北京海伦网络信息科技有限公司"，为海伦钢琴提供信息技术支持。

### 3. 二代主导：从智能钢琴到培训学校

2014年，陈氏父子经过慎重沟通后决定，大方向由陈海伦负责，具体事务则由陈朝峰负责。陈朝峰成立了"海伦艺术教育投资有限公司"，在继续发展智能化教具的同时对艺术教育产业进行探索，这对海伦钢琴来说是从制造业到服务业的产业提升。陈氏父子认为，中国艺术教育培训市场仍有空白，智能钢琴不仅可以承担便民娱乐功能，还可以承担钢琴教学功能。在这一理念的指导下，他们尝试建立音乐培训学校，向艺术教育市场进军。中国艺术启蒙教育市场的空白让智能钢琴有了用武之地。对现在的孩子来说，学习钢琴不仅时间长，而且学习过程特别枯燥。这长此以往会导致孩子积攒厌学情绪。但如果钢琴学习时间较短，学习效果又不明显。此外，早期钢琴快速考证考级的风气使钢琴教育忽视了最根本的基础乐理教育，而这恰是钢琴教育不可忽视的问题。现在越来越多的家长意识到了这一问题，愿意让孩子接受更多的艺术熏陶，学习基础乐理知识，而不再一味地追求钢琴考级，这些转变给智能化教具的发展提供了良好的外部环境。

智能钢琴向智能化教具方向发展，为海伦钢琴发展教育培训奠定了基础。一方面，陈朝峰团队开发了能实现一对多教学培训的App，不仅降低了学习成本，还通过动画和教学互动激发了孩子的学习兴趣。海伦钢琴的创新之处是对孩子进行指弹教育，通过不同顺序的琴键指示灯对孩子进行纠错辅导，通过软件陪练，真正做到了对孩子的私人辅导。另一方面，海伦钢琴聘请北京师范大学的教授指导编写课程，并将课程应用于网络教学；同时海伦钢琴还在逐步筹建智能钢琴教室、音乐培训学校，其与宁波市的高校合作成立音乐学校试点，与中央音乐学院签约共同开发课程内容。

海伦钢琴两代领导人的努力推动着海伦钢琴从一个小小的钢琴配件厂发展为如今的行业龙头企业。在发展过程中，海伦钢琴不仅实现了组织的转型发展，也顺利地完成了家族传承。

## 【案例来源】

孔令贺，陈士慧，倪嘉婕．海伦钢琴：家族企业创业式传承［J］．企业管理，2021（11）：81-85.

彭新敏，史慧敏．从"跑龙套"到"唱主角"：海伦奏响美妙琴音［J］．清华管理评论，2020（Z2）：128-134.

## 【案例问题】

1. 根据"一代奠基：从五金'码克'到整琴制造"这部分内容，分析海伦钢琴的战略管理过程。
2. 海伦钢琴在三次转型中分别采用了什么样的企业层战略和竞争战略？
3. 根据案例内容分析战略领导的重要作用。

## 【分析提示】

1. 战略管理过程包含六个步骤，分别为识别组织当前的使命、目标和战略，进行外部环境分析，进行组织内部分析，制定战略，实施战略和评估结果。在这部分内容中，陈海伦的战略管理目标是进行钢琴整琴制造。通过内外部环境分析可以发现，为了避免和国内老牌厂商竞争，陈海伦采取了用配件养钢琴的策略，并将生产的钢琴全部销往欧洲，这种做法也可以更好地检验产品的质量。

2. 企业层战略是决定组织从事或想从事什么业务，以及想如何从事这些业务的战略，主要包括成长战略、稳定战略和更新战略。竞争战略是决定组织在每种业务上如何展开竞争的战略,主要包括成本领先战略、差异化战略和聚焦战略。在企业战略层面:①从五金"码克"到整琴制造,海伦钢琴采取的是成长战略中的纵向一体化战略,即通过前向一体化实现成长;②从整琴制造到智能钢琴和从智能钢琴到培训学校,海伦钢琴采取的是成长战略中的多元化战略。在竞争战略层面:①从五金"码克"到整琴制造,海伦钢琴采取的是差异化战略,即以质量展开竞争,并且选择了海外市场;②从整琴制造到智能钢琴,海伦钢琴采取的是差异化战略和聚焦战略,即聚焦于钢琴市场上的智能钢琴产品,并成立全资子公司支持技术研发;③从智能钢琴到培训学校,海伦钢琴采取的是差异化战略,即开发钢琴教学功能,并从智能钢琴向智能化教具方向发展。

【企业层战略】

3.战略领导是指高层管理者预测、展望、保持灵活性和战略性的思考以及与组织中其他人共同发动变革而为组织创造光明未来的能力。高层管理者提供有效的战略领导的八个关键维度是:确定组织的目标或愿景,培育和保持组织的核心竞争力,开发组织的人力资本,创造和保持一种强有力的组织文化,维持和拓展组织的各种关系,通过询问敏锐的问题和质疑各种假设来对主流观点进行重组,强调有道德的组织决策和决策时间,建立张弛有度的组织管控体系。本案例中的父子二人均能够清晰地描绘组织的目标和愿景,能够通过内外部环境分析找到适合企业的战略。

# 案例 9

## 风华的组织结构变革

## 【案例正文】

  风华物业服务有限公司（以下简称风华）于1991年8月在广州成立，它是一家由自然人投资的民营企业，业务涉及写字楼物业、政企后勤物业、城市综合体物业、商业广场物业、居住物业、公共交通体系服务、城区综合服务、公用事业服务、道路保洁等。近年来，风华的市场版图从广州扩展到了全国20个省份的39个城市。在风华高速发展的同时，风华董事长、第一大股东白总发现，公司规模越来越大，似乎什么都做，但特色却不鲜明，专业化能力也不足。随着组织规模日益扩大，以及业务类型逐渐多元化，风华原有的组织结构已无法适应高速发展的需要。2018年年底，风华确立了做城市服务商的新定位。但在新定位下应该如何进行组织变革？针对这一问题，风华管理层有不同的意见。

### 1. 专业化还是区域化

  在30余年的发展历程中，风华始终保持着对外部环境的敏感性和灵活性。风华在创立之初主要定位于老旧住宅物业服务，后来定位于酒店式物业管理，再后来，随着广州房地产市场的不断升温，外地地产商的大量涌入，白总带领风华开拓写字楼业务，实现了从住宅业务向写字楼业务的大转型，自此，写字楼业务成为风华的招牌业务。但之后写字楼供应过剩以及物业费回收困难等问题频频出现，又迫使风华从写字楼业务向城市服务业务转型。以政府楼宇、公众物业为主的城市服务业务在风华业务结构中的比重逐年上升，成为风华的主要业务。

  目前风华的管理模式是以各区域分公司自主开拓为主，职能部门统一协调为辅（见图1），由总公司对下属分公司、子公司进行绩效考核和管理。

  风华董事长、第一大股东白总认为，目前风华的组织结构问题太多了。随着每年开发的项目数量持续增长，风华面临的风险也将与日俱增，基层员工数也会随之增加，如果一个项目出问题，就会波及风华的其他项目。因此，组织结构应该朝专业化的方向发展，但是目前采取的区域化发展模式也有很多优点，是风华高速成长的重要支撑，改变组织结构将会增加成本与风险。

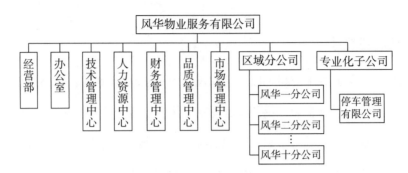

**图 1　风华目前的组织结构**

风华总经理赵总认为，由于目前风华只有一家道路停车管理的专业化公司，其余的都是区域分公司，因此专业化发展较难实现资源共享。而且区域分公司的员工对当地市场非常熟悉，如果由专业化公司负责这些市场的拓展工作，势必造成极大的人力浪费。

作为风华第三大股东的王总认为，由于风华一直以来都鼓励区域分公司积极拓展市场，员工的收入与其所承接的项目总量紧密相关，因此很容易形成"山头主义"，人才的轮岗机制也无法推行。成立专业化公司可以更好地对各类业务进行独立核算，也更有利于明确资源的分配。另外，目前没有一家区域分公司在全力主攻一个业务领域，这就造成公司的专业化能力很弱，而且对同一个项目，不同分公司的管理方式千差万别，公司亟须提升专业竞争优势。风华目前利润低、成本高，增值业务挖掘难度大，因此需要对不同类别的业务进行深入的专业化研究。

近几年，外部竞争环境发生了巨大的变化，风华的专业竞争力明显不足。一方面，大量的大型物业公司纷纷将触角转向城市公共服务领域。比如开元物业提出了城市运营服务商的企业定位；碧桂园启动了城市共生计划，并与遵义、衡水、西昌等十余个城市达成战略合作。另一方面，一些依托互联网、高科技的"小而美"的专业化公司市场定位十分清晰。与这些竞争者相比，风华在专业服务、增值业务拓展、项目经营等方面都不占优势。

**2. 论证会的召开**

由于风华的管理层始终无法作出选择，因此管理层决定召开一次公开的论证会，邀请区域分公司经理参与讨论，希望在论证会上，各方能够对组织结构的选择问题提出具体建议，并充分讨论其利弊。

论证会以风华组织结构的选择为主题如期召开。白总强调了召开此次论证会的意义："随着公司规模的不断扩张，原有的组织结构难以适应公司的发展需求。目前公司存在的管理分散、上下级之间沟通不足等问题制约了公司未来的发展。因此需要经过充分论证，从而选出与公司实际情况相匹配并能顺应市场发展趋势的组织结构模式。"

风华六分公司经理罗总认为："目前公司的区域化组织结构还是有很大优势的。由于区域分公司的各个项目是在一个区域内，因此，物业人员在不同项目之间的调剂非常灵活。比如写字楼是周一到周五繁忙、周末空闲，而公园景区则正好相反，那么写字楼的物业人员就可以与公园景区的物业人员相互协调，从而降低人工成本。就新市场的开拓而言，公司实行的是谁先申报谁先占领的激励政策，这极大地调动了各分公司的积极性，这也是区域化组织结构的优势。同时，区域化发展使得各分公司在当地市场经营中积累了很多经验，更容易接到项目……"

而风华七分公司的胡总却非常赞同专业化，他认为目前最困难的是风华定位为城市服务商以后，对城市服务商的理解却不够，采用的还是以前的管理方式。由于风华没有上游房产做支撑，完全是从专业的物业公司发展起来的，因此专业化水平是风华参与竞争的关键。当然，专业化的划分意味着风华原有的区域化组织结构模式将被打破，而这会涉及很多利益问题。

目前在做专业化公司试点的停车管理有限公司负责人杨总认为："虽然将各区域的项目划给专业化公司进行管理会涉及较大的利润分配问题，但这并不是成立专业化公司的障碍。比如，停车管理有限公司虽然还在起步阶段，但管理模式已经比较清晰了。因为专业化公司的指导和监管是需要成本的，所以肯定要向区域分公司收取一定的费用。只要公司的整体架构确定好，就不会产生利润分配的问题。"

风华三分公司的马总非常反对专业化。他认为目前风华核心成员的文化层次不高，大多数管理人员都是从基层一步一个脚印走出来的。因此目前风华还不太适合去做比较大的跨越。而且专业化服务对公司管理水平要求较高，与风华目前的实际情况不相符。不管是在传统的物业管理领域，还是在城市服务领域，风华都不够专业。风华虽然提出了城市服务战略理念，但是还主要停留在概念层面。

各分公司经理提出的观点都有一定的道理，但是关于选择专业化组织结构还是区域化组织结构的意见仍然没有得到统一。这主要是因为已有的结构虽然存在问题，但也有优势，而其他类型的组织结构虽有优势，但也不见得能让风华发展得一帆风顺。会议虽然结束了，但问题并未得到解决，到底应该选择哪种组织结构才能保证风华实现顺利发展呢？

## 【案例问题】

1. 案例中所提到的区域化和专业化分别对应哪种组织结构设计？
2. 区域化和专业化组织结构设计分别有哪些优缺点？
3. 结合案例，说明影响组织结构设计的因素有哪些。
4. 如果你是白总，你认为哪种组织结构更适合现阶段风华的发展？请你为风华设计合适的组织结构。

## 【分析提示】

【组织设计的部门化】

1. 组织结构有多种类型，包括职能型、矩阵型、事业部型、区域型等。案例中的区域化是指按照不同的市场范围划分组织部门，专业化是指根据不同的业务内容划分横向组织部门。

2. 每种组织结构设计都有优势和劣势，这是由不同的组织结构特点所决定的。比如，专业化组织结构设计可提升管理效率，但却容易产生较高的官僚成本。

3.影响组织结构设计的因素主要有六个,包括工作专业化、部门化、命令链、控制跨度、集权与分权及正规化。

4.可以根据影响组织结构设计的因素,对案例资料进行分析并设计相应的组织结构。

## 案例 10

# 恩凯的人力资源管理

## 【案例正文】

2005年，为了促进纺织品贸易，中国降低了部分纺织品的出口关税，并且当时中国的劳动力成本相对较低，这些都为纺织品外贸企业带来了发展空间。正是看到了这一市场机遇，在宁波一家纺织品外贸企业工作了十余年的沈功灿果断地辞去了副总经理职务，创建了以女装为主打产品的宁波恩凯控股有限公司（以下简称恩凯）。在外贸企业积累的工作经验，以及积攒下来的资金及人脉，为沈功灿的创业打下了牢固的基础。在恩凯的整个发展过程中，贸易不仅是整个集团发展的"排头兵"，也为恩凯在其他领域的发展提供了初始资金、培养和输送了大量人才。

### 1. 从单纯贸易到"贸工教一体"：挑选和培养自己的骨干员工

在创业初期，恩凯以单一的纺织品贸易为主，主要通过先联系客户获取订单，再联系代加工工厂生产产品，最后如期将货物交送给客户这种赚取中间利润差价的模式获取利润。作为曾经的最佳销售，沈功灿在外贸营销方面的丰富经验是他带领团队攻克市场的关键。恩凯源源不断地获得订单，并进入快速成长阶段。恩凯一方面大量招揽外贸市场的开拓人员，另一方面以寻找创业合伙人的心态筛选培养外贸骨干员工。在这一阶段，事业留人、文化留人、制度保障是恩凯对外贸骨干进行管理的核心。

随着企业的不断发展壮大，恩凯的客户越来越多，供应商也达到了数十家。但在订单交付的过程中，恩凯与代加工工厂及供应商之间的沟通时常出现误会，导致其对客户提出的需求未能及时响应，恩凯因此遭受了不小的损失。随着国内各行业生产成本的逐渐上升，继续从事单一的纺织品贸易已经不能满足恩凯快速发展的需求了。要解决这个问题，沈功灿认为只有尽快拥有自建工厂或联盟工厂，才能极大地提升恩凯的综合竞争力。但建设工厂与单纯做贸易有所不同，自建工厂对骨干技术工人的需求量非常大，对此，沈功灿想到了"贸工教一体"经营模式。由恩凯冠名赞助的"NKM（恩凯）时装技术高级研究班"在浙江纺织职业技术学院举办，恩凯将骨干技术工人送去培训班进行免费的定向技术培训。工人学成归来后，首选是回到自建工厂或联盟工厂反哺企业，同时他们获得了更高的经济收入并提升了人力资源价值。由此，恩凯形成了技术人员继续培养与工厂可持续发展的联动模式。

"贸工教一体"经营模式提高了恩凯对市场需求的反应能力，而且拥有自己的工厂有助于恩凯的相关部门直接核算成本并进行品质管控。同时，恩凯还可以更好地把自己的经营理念直接传递给原料供应商和基层员工，起到模范引领作用，从而打造出一个良好的、稳定的生产供应链。随着纺织高校教师、公司设计师、工厂工人、上下游利益相关方的合作越来越紧密，恩凯"贸工教一体"经营模式逐渐走向成熟。强有力的基层员工为恩凯赢得了更多客户的青睐和发展机会，恩凯在纺织品外贸领域得到快速发展。

**2. 从代工到原厂委托设计再到自主品牌生产：建立国际化设计师队伍**

在发展初期，恩凯主要以代工方式从事纺织品贸易，即利用品牌方的核心技术以及设计理念进行代工生产，再由品牌方买断这些商品并贴上品牌标签进行销售。代工生产是发达地区的企业通过转移加工工厂获得更大利润空间的手段，但同时也为欠发达地区带来了发展机会。虽然代工生产的利润和发展空间较小，但企业的整体结构会相对稳定。另外，代工生产也能让企业获得较好的锻炼和发展机会，并在这个过程中积攒大量稳定的品牌客户。

随着竞争对手增多、客户需求发生变化，以及企业自身的发展需求发生变化，许多外贸企业纷纷由最初的代工转向原厂委托设计。这是因为自主设计能够大大提升企业的综合竞争力。原厂委托设计生产主要是指生产商设计出某些产品供客户选择及订购，这些产品生产完成后会贴上客户的品牌标签进行销售。在原厂委托设计生产过程中，生产商具备了更多的主动权，其企业竞争力和议价能力大大提高了。从代工到原厂委托设计，不仅是时代发展所驱，更是恩凯积极应对行业发展变化的明智选择。

由于原厂委托设计的生产商需要具备产品设计开发能力，因此恩凯需要配备优秀的设计师团队。土耳其地处亚洲和欧洲的交界地带，在接受西方文化的同时能够兼容东方文化元素，对时尚的接受力强，接受速度也很快；而且土耳其距离欧洲较近，在土耳其设立办事处有利于与客户进行接洽，提高订单成交率；相比于欧洲其他国家而言，土耳其无论是设计师的薪资水平还是办公场所的租赁费用都相对较低，在土耳其办事处设置展厅可以突显企业实力。因此，恩凯选择在土耳其的伊斯坦布尔建立设计工作室，从当地招募具有欧洲服装经验的专业服装设计师，专门针对西方客户设计产品，再由位于中国的工厂加工制造。

就纺织领域的外贸企业而言，其最终的发展方向就是能够成功地转变为自主品牌生产商。因为，一方面，如果仅仅做代工的话，附加值较低，企业的发展空间有限；另一方面，拥有自身的品牌，不管是从利润角度还是从综合竞争力角度来说，企业的实力都会获得很大的提升。恩凯正是看到了这一点，利用在代工和原厂委托设计阶段积累的生产经验和技术等资源，筹划建立自己的品牌，逐步向自主品牌生产转型。

**3. 海外投资与全球范围资源整合：寻觅国际化人才**

随着国内劳动力、土地、水电等生产成本的上升，恩凯开始进行全球设计与生产的布局。恩凯逐渐将代工部分转向了东南亚等劳动力成本较低且原材料较丰富的地区；对于设计要求较高的中高端产品，或者款式新颖且交货周期较短的产品，则交由土耳其的工作室设计，并安排位于东南亚的工厂进行生产；国内的总公司负责全球资源配置和关系协调，尽可能充分利用不同国家的设计优势或生产优势。

为满足这套国际化运行机制，恩凯强调要整合国际化资源、培养国际化人才。沈功灿认为，国际化人才稀缺和招聘困难一直以来制约着外贸企业的成长。由于土耳其地处欧亚大陆交界地带，因此位于土耳其的工作室更容易聘请到具有西方背景和先进理念的国际设计师，这些设计师设计的产品也更符合欧美客户的需求。

相较以往其他企业重金邀请这些国际化人才到中国工作或者进行项目合作，恩凯根据国际化人才的偏好，选择在土耳其设立自有工作室，获得了一批稳定的国际设计师。同时，其国内设计师也会与土耳其设计师保持一定程度的沟通。通过生产、设计与投资的国际布局，恩凯进行了全球范围的资源整合，这不仅增加了企业的利润，还降低了运营成本，有效提高了企业竞争力。

## 【案例问题】

1. 试解释人力资源管理对恩凯的重要性。
2. 恩凯的战略转型与人力资源管理是如何有效结合的？
3. 简述用来留住高绩效优秀员工的各种战略。

## 【分析提示】

1. 人力资源管理重要的原因有三个：第一，人力资源能够成为竞争优势的重要来源；第二，人力资源管理是组织战略的重要组成部分；第三，组织对待员工的方式会对组织绩效产生显著影响。可结合具体案例内容，分析恩凯是如何通过有效的人力资源管理获得创业成功的。主要涉及的知识点有人力资源的定义、性质和重要性。

2. 根据战略性人力资源管理理论，分析恩凯三次战略转型过程中，人力资源管理是如何匹配企业战略转型需要的。例如，恩凯在创业初期将骨干员工视为合伙人，打造"贸工教一体"经营模式，努力提高基层员工的技术水平；在原厂委托设计生产阶段高薪聘请国际设计师等。主要涉及的知识点有员工的招聘和甄选、薪酬管理和福利计划、当代人力资源管理。

【留住高绩效员工的策略】

3. 恩凯根据员工表现出的工作技能和综合能力向员工支付薪酬，通过对员工的工龄、工作绩效、工作种类，企业所在行业，企业的类型、地理位置、盈利能力和规模等方面进行综合考虑，设计出完善的薪酬福利体系来留住高绩效员工。主要涉及的知识点有影响员工薪酬和福利的因素、基于技能的薪酬体系等。

## 案例 11

## 忘不了服饰的领导实践

## 【案例正文】

湖南省忘不了万德融和服饰集团（以下简称忘不了服饰）是罗美元于1984年创立的，它是国内最早将西裤进行规模化生产的企业，也是中国纺织行业竞争力百强企业和中国服装行业百强企业，主要生产西服、西裤、衬衫、羽绒服、风衣等产品。2014年，家族第二代刘佳玟正式接手，她以研发创新和员工激励为核心，致力于推动忘不了服饰成为百年品牌。目前，忘不了服饰实施多品牌化、集团化的经营战略，旗下拥有WONBLY忘不了（商务男装）、WONBLYlady（时尚职业女装）、WONBLYyoung（时尚休闲电子商务装）、CHOCY超世洋服（高级定制）及团购定制职业装五大品牌业务。

### 1. 创始人罗美元：真情换真心

1984年，罗美元凭着熟练的缝纫剪裁技术，聚集了一群心灵手巧的姐妹，办起了宁乡首家民营服装厂。建厂伊始，罗美元就确立了"以质量求生存，以信誉求发展"的企业发展理念，对每件产品均精工细作，力求质量过硬。作为厂长兼设计师和推销员，她每天骑自行车去40千米外的长沙进原料，还要驮着产品去长沙推销。在同厂姐妹们的共同努力下，工厂日益兴旺，在十年后成功搬迁新址。新工厂需要新名字，罗美元希望新名字跟大家有关，因为工厂有今天是员工们共同努力的结果，这些年员工们点点滴滴的帮助都让她忘不了。由此，忘不了服饰诞生了，并发展为如今享誉全国的服装品牌。

自1994年开始，忘不了服饰进入快速成长期，管理是这位自称"没上过什么学"的企业家需要从零做起的事情。罗美元认为，自己完全是凭人格魅力在管理公司，用真情建设公司，以真情打动员工。在当时的800多名员工中，80%是她从各地招来的下岗女工和待业青年。在员工培养方面，她总是以大姐的身份，与她们促膝谈心，以自己的经历引导她们，帮助她们重新找到人生目标；当员工犯错时，她像母亲一样循循善诱，一遍又一遍、不厌其烦地跟对方解释，体现出柔性管理的大智慧。

在罗美元看来，好公司应该是一所好学校，能让员工时刻得到知识的浇灌、感受文化的熏陶，与公司共同成长。为此，忘不了服饰建立了员工书屋和文体活动室，定期订阅报纸和专业书刊；定期举行公司中高管读书会，由管理者带头阅读，引导员工学习现代管理知识和专业技术，提升员工的综合素质，促进公司创新能力建设；举办技术工人技能培训班，以企业职工培训中心为平台，大力开展技能培训。

2014年，罗美元发起了"元基金"项目，忘不了服饰每卖出一件衣服，就拿出一元钱做公益。该基金主要致力于资助贫困学生、关爱孤寡老人、赞助中国航天事业、帮扶困难职工和救济重大自然灾害中的灾民等。比如，公司每年评比出7名最美孝心员工，并每人奖励1万元；与中国航天基金会联合设立"忘不了·航天奖学金"，激励青年人勤于钻研、开拓创新，为中国航空航天技术和国防现代化建设储备力量；在重阳节为夏铎铺镇敬老院的老人们送钱送米送衣服，问寒问暖问忧愁；年终会特地为生产一线员工的父母写一封信，并委托员工带去新年慰问金，表达对其父母的敬重，感谢他们承担家务，让员工全心地投入工作。在罗美元的领导下，员工们完全融入忘不了服饰的真情文化之中，深深感到公司就是自己的家。

**2. 继承人刘佳玟：让员工幸福生活**

2014年，刘佳玟从母亲罗美元手上接过掌舵旗帜，这意味着这家知名企业正式进入传承期。在如何管理员工的问题上，两代领导者体现出的风格各具特色。刘佳玟认为，她领导的团队是一群年轻人，这些人文化水平高，思想开放，创新意识强，个人意识也较强。她要做的是在工作上给予员工成长的时间，培养他们的抗压能力，让员工通过完成任务来不断产生个人价值从而提升企业价值；在生活上满足他们对精神、文化方面的需求，提高员工的幸福指数，从而达到帮助公司招人、留人、发展人的目的。

上任伊始，刘佳玟提出要以平等关系为基础重新打造管理架构。一是完善"集体决策，分级管理"的管理机制，充分调动高层管理人员的工作热情；二是将看板管理引入高层管理；三是要求各部门回顾总结工作经验，从而寻找改进机会，制订相应措施，以标准化的方式制订工作规范。刘佳玟认为，公司为员工提供的不仅仅是一份工作,更是一份事业,是能让员工充分发挥聪明才智和创造力的舞台。

刘佳玟将提升员工在公司工作的幸福指数作为留住人才、吸引人才的关键。比如,根据年轻人的喜好,不断改善符合年轻员工性格特点的配套生活设施,设立员工健身房、瑜伽室、活动室;每年举行员工运动会,开展多种形式的兴趣活动;为员工宿舍开通光纤网络,满足年轻员工工作之余的娱乐需求。这一系列努力使公司的文化理念由原来的"快乐学习、快乐工作、快乐生活"转变为"幸福生活"。快乐工作的员工能传递积极的能量,把产品做得更好,最终也会让顾客的感受更好。

**3. 尾声:百年企业**

忘不了服饰在两代领导者的努力下,逐渐从一个传统制造企业向高新技术企业转变,从一般消费品生产商向时尚消费品生产商转变,从一个员工的就业平台向员工与企业共发展的致富平台转变。这家中国企业的百年品牌梦,正通过扎实稳步推进品牌建设,做出真正有品质、有品位,让顾客认可的产品来逐步实现。

【案例来源】

蔡力强,毛吉元. 历史的传承与担当——访湖南忘不了服饰有限公司80后总经理刘佳玟 [J]. 中国纺织, 2012 (8): 130–132.

张炯宇,张国军,张晓辉. 用真情裁剪人生——访全国人大代表、湖南忘不了服饰有限公司董事长罗美元 [J]. 华商, 2011 (2): 32–33.

【案例问题】

1. 根据忘不了服饰的领导实践,分析管理者为什么应当成为领导者。

2. 根据马斯洛需要层次论,分析创始人罗美元的"真情换真心"领导方式和刘佳玟的"让员工幸福生活"领导方式分别满足了员工的什么需求?

3. 请用领导权变理论分析,为什么在罗美元"真情换真心"的领导方式已经取得成功的情况下,刘佳玟还要改变领导方式?

**【分析提示】**

1. 管理者应该成为领导者,是因为领导者是能够影响他人并拥有管理职权的人。领导是领导者所做的事情,是带领并影响某个群体实现目标的一个过程。从本案例可以看出,两代领导者根据各自的性格特征,选择成为不同类型的领导者,但是这两种类型领导者的共同点是,既关注任务又关注员工。忘不了服饰的两代领导者均能设身处地地为员工考虑,将员工的利益作为决策参考因素,赢得了员工的支持和爱戴,从而使员工能够更加高效地完成组织任务。主要涉及的知识点有领导的定义和领导的重要性。

【马斯洛需要层次论】

2. 马斯洛认为人有五个层次的需求,分别为生理需求、安全需求、社交需求、尊重需求和自我实现需求。马斯洛认为一个需求层次必须得到实质的满足后,才会激活下一个层次的需求。领导者应先判断员工所处的需求层次,再采取相应的措施来激励员工为满足自身的需求而努力工作。例如,罗美元注重满足员工的社交需求,而刘佳玫更侧重于满足员工的自我实现需求。

3. 领导权变理论认为,任务导向的领导方式在极端有利和极端不利的情境下表现最佳,而关系导向的领导方式在适度有利的情境下表现最佳。本案例可以根据领导权变理论,讨论任务导向的领导方式和关系导向的领导方式的关系,分析两代领导者各自的领导力特质。

## 案例 12

# 立拓能源的创业团队

## 【案例正文】

如何组织建立新创企业的专业化的创业团队？创业者应如何提高创业团队的效率？对于这些问题，立拓能源的陈都在进行创业之前就已有了自己独特的看法。陈都想通过组建专业化的创业团队对生物质能源进行研究和推广。创业以来，陈都带领核心研发团队，在技术上打破传统瓶颈，成功地将秸秆、木屑等农林废弃物生产成可取代石油基燃料的生物质再生能源，目前已生产出生物柴油、重质油、生物沥青、生物碳材料等多种产品，以相对较低的成本实现了新能源行业难以实现的目标，这些产品的经济、环境效益显著。

### 1. 选定创业项目

21世纪初，由于人们开始意识到了环境问题，街面上随处可见保护环境的标语。在这种氛围的熏陶下，一颗"环保"的种子在还是小学生的陈都心里生根发芽。长大后的陈都对环保热情不减，她在上大学期间经常和同学一起爬山捡垃圾，也一直希望有机会能参加联合国的公益项目。

陈都在美国加州大学读书时接触到了生物质能源新技术，她发现生物质能源已经是北美非常普遍的技术产业，但是在中国并没有得到产业化，如果能将现有的一些技术整合，针对中国特定的原材料进行参数调整，让中国大量存在的农林废弃物成为石化资源替代品，必然有巨大的市场潜力。对于陈都来说，创建一家生物质能源公司既可以保护环境，又可以产生价值，何乐而不为？

生物质能源新技术的研发者是陈都学校的一位教授，由于前景光明，技术刚一问世便有许多公司前来寻求合作。如何在众多强大的竞争者中脱颖而出并获得技术的使用权，对陈都而言无疑是一个巨大的挑战。陈都坚信创业项目是不会自己找上门来的，一定要主动去争取。利用同校的便利，陈都多次登门与教授沟通。然而跨国合作并不是一件容易的事情，教授有着诸多疑虑。陈都告知教授她自幼的环保梦想和她的愿望：在中国创建一家清洁能源企业，为社会作出更大的贡献。教授深受感动，最终带着技术加入生物质能源的应用研发项目。

### 2. 构建团队

然而，仅有技术是远远不够的，一个专业化的创业团队才是创业成功的关键。陈都本身拥有出众的表达能力，她从不会因为要接触大型企业的相关负责人而蹑手蹑脚，而是会通过自己的人际交往经验，循序渐进地让对方敞开心扉。凭借努力，陈都获得了合作商 1000 万元的注资。同时，她凭借优秀的社交能力，吸引了一批具有海外背景的高层次人才，为立拓能源打造了一支顶尖的国际化团队。团队成员有专攻生物技术和有机化学研究的专家，有从事 20 多年化工技术研发的总工程师，有熟悉新能源产品销售和服务的市场人才，等等。2017 年，从美国毕业回国的陈都带着最新的生物质转化技术和专业化团队创办了立拓能源。

立拓能源作为一家新企业，无论在技术上还是在管理上，都具有"新生弱性"，但陈都优秀的领导力和团队的合作力为这家新企业带来了勃勃生机。陈都在大学时期专攻数学，具有扎实的专业基础，对于数据模型、经济模型等建模知识烂熟于心。新能源的提炼、回收等都需要精确的配比做支撑。在进行能源提炼前，陈都会根据专业知识先创建前期的架构，将不同实验数据录入架构当中，这些技术手段逐渐成为企业的核心优势。同时，长期合作的同事之间也逐渐形成了默契，在项目实施过程中，不同的文化背景并未成为阻碍，反而成为本土工程师和国外工程师相互激发新思路的源泉，陈都也充分尊重这些专业人士的意见和建议。团队在关键技术攻关上保持高效沟通，共同做决策，攻克了一系列技术难题。

一直以来，陈都及其团队的目标都是为环保事业做贡献，因此公司希望开发出市场上少有的清洁能源以替代高成本、重污染的石化产品，并在参数整理方面走在行业前端。共同的目标极大地激发了团队的工作热情。比如，在工作时，团队成员毫无怨言，经常连续通宵数天监测数据，以防运行过程中出现数据差错。团队成员齐心协力，为实现从生物质能源中提炼具有高附加值的石油焦的目标而努力。

团队的长期努力得到了回报。立拓能源在台州工厂所进行的中试操作流程与物质转化都已较为成熟，在指定设备参与、工艺控制措施等方面，形成了独有的生物焦工艺包和数据库，具备生物质燃料的规模化条件，可以实现石焦油的小批量生产。未来立拓能源的产品可应用于石墨电极与锂电池负极材料，是具有高附加值和市场高度需求的产品，也是立拓能源的创业团队经历多次商业模式优化和技术研发调整，不断摸索想要获得的产品。

### 3. 尾声

回想创业经历，陈都认为，人力资源是企业的核心竞争力。未来立拓能源的阶段性目标是引入资本，支持中试提产和试点合作，以技术输出或合作建厂等方式开展大规模生产，努力将企业的产品从中试阶段推入产业化阶段。

【案例问题】

1. 结合案例内容，分析立拓能源创始人在组建创业团队前做了哪些准备？
2. 根据案例内容，分析立拓能源的创业团队有哪些特征？
3. 立拓能源创始人是如何提高创业团队效率的？

【分析提示】

1. 本案例可以根据领导者特质理论，从领导者能力、个性品质、外部环境影响等方面对立拓能源创始人所做的创业准备进行分析。以立拓能源为例，其创始人在选择项目阶段花费了大量的精力，根据个人兴趣和既有机会反复考察，最终才确定目标并加以实施。此外，领导者需要判断群体或团队所处的创业阶段，因为每个阶段涉及不同的事项和行为。例如，形成阶段是群体发展的第一个阶段，因此领导者需要帮助成员加入群体并定义群体的目的、结构和领导方式。主要涉及的知识点有团队管理、团队发展阶段等。

2. 创业团队的特征包括：共同分担领导角色；承担个人责任和团队责任；具有特定的团队目标；会议以开放式讨论和合力解决问题为特征；通过评估集体工作结果衡量工作绩效；工作由集体决定，由团队成员共同完成。以立拓能源为例，其团队坚持合作共赢，在复杂的国际化背景下，也尽量保持开放性沟通和共同决策。主要涉及的知识点有团队特征、团队绩效影响因素等。

  3.提高创业团队效率的方法有：团队拥有一位强有力的、掌握主导权的领导者；个人承担责任；团队目标与组织目标相同；个人独立完成工作；会议效率高；工作先由团队领导者决定，再分配给团队成员；等等。可以从专业人才选聘、团队管理等方面对"立拓能源创始人是如何提高创业团队效率的"进行分析。主要涉及的知识点有团队特征、愿景、团队目标、团队成员角色分配等。

【团队有效性】

## 案例 13

### 宁波海辰大药店的店长激励

## 【案例正文】

1999年，中专毕业的小徐在机缘巧合下来到济南的一家民营药厂做文职工作，并由此进入了医药行业。由于小徐工作出色，两年后她就被调到销售部担任药厂的销售员。

2003年，小徐来到宁波，在开心人大药房站柜销售。开心人大药房是宁波首家采用开架购买模式的药店，在这里，小徐不仅学会了销售技巧，而且对药店消费者的消费行为有了非常深刻的理解。她开始留心观察药店的经营模式和管理特点，并逐渐萌生了自己开药店的想法。

2010年，小徐的丈夫退伍复员，夫妻两人决定自己创业，于是开设了海辰大药店。凭借小徐在医药行业多年积累下来的销售经验，以及夫妻两人的努力，药店不久就实现了盈利。

### 1. 挑选店长

2014年，小徐夫妻开了第四家药店。这时候，小徐夫妻明显感觉精力不够，无法时刻对各个店面进行严格的质量管控和跟踪管理。药店在运营过程中，经常出现员工虚报营业收入的情况。但由于小徐经常不在药店，也不能天天提醒员工不能虚报，让员工感到不信任、不尊重，因此，寻找合适的店长并有效地激励他们管理好药店，成了当务之急。

一个药店，至少需要配备一个职业药师和一个助理药师，再根据店面的大小和客流量情况，配备销售员、收银员和店长。很多小药店为了节约成本，往往只配备两个药师，由这两个药师分别兼任收银员和店长。销售能力是店长应该具备的核心能力。具备合格的药学知识和良好销售能力的员工，能够把消费者的最终消费额增加到其计划购买额度的3~5倍。在零售药店，相较男性员工，女性员工往往更擅长与消费者聊天，向消费者推荐药品。所以小徐最终选定的店长几乎都是积极努力的女性。

**2. 员工激励措施**

在员工激励方面,小徐夫妻采用了非常灵活的方案。比如,小徐夫妻根据原有的年销售额设定基准销售额,员工完成基准销售额就可以拿到基本工资,超过基准销售额部分按比例获得提成,即采用"多干多得"的激励措施来提高业绩。另外,他们在不影响销售的情况下,尽可能缩减员工数量。例如,原来有3个员工,现在缩减到2个,相当于把3个人的工资发给2个人,但是实际上工资总额比雇用3个人时要低一点儿,而且因为工资提高了,预先设定的目标指标也可以适当提高。这样做的结果就是企业成本降低了,而员工工资、目标指标和员工的积极性都提高了。

**3. 独特的店长承包模式**

此外,小徐自创了一种独特的店长承包模式。比如,对于一家小徐认为可以赚20万元的药店,由小徐承担房租并配备好执业药师、助理药师各一名,如果最终由执业药师做承包店长,那么日常开支就由店长负责,小徐年终时拿到她预期的20万元,其他多赚的部分归店长。这种模式有一个难题:每个药店都需要一定量的库存药品来维持日常运营,而大部分店长的经济实力不允许他们把库存买下来,如果由承包的店长免费接管库存,那么在小徐无法监管店长日常运营行为的情况下,就存在店长转卖库存并携带变现款逃跑的风险。小徐通过"分期盘"的方式解决了这个难题。如果承包当日盘点的库存价值10万元,店长可以在半年内分期购买,那么在承包的前半年,店长可以用每个月的销售额支付给小徐1万~2万元。这样既解决了小徐的担忧,又为经济实力不足的承包店长提供了启动资金。同时,承包前期的分期购买也增加了店长的违约成本,可以促使店长更加用心地经营。当店长因意外原因不再承包时,根据协议,小徐也会以"分期盘"的方式用半年时间再把库存盘回来。这样一来,主动权就一直掌握在小徐手里。这种模式在保证库存不会被恶意转移的同时,能够激励店长为增加营业收入而全力以赴。小徐在3家药店试行了4年店长承包模式,效果非常好。在基本不牵扯小徐精力的情况下,3家药店的业绩都有明显的提升,小徐每年都拿到了预期的回报,3家药店的店长的经济状况也有了明显的改善。

**4. 在新的行业变革下,原店长承包模式面临挑战**

(1) 个体药店恶性竞争导致利润空间下降

宁波以个体经营的药店数量在全市药店数量中的占比非常高,在新冠疫情暴发前,这一比值高达60%～70%,这一局面的产生有其历史原因。宁波个体药店的所有者在供销社改制前,大多在供销社担任执业药师,具备专业知识且与医院及医药公司有着良好的人际关系。在供销社改制后,他们以个体经营者的身份承接了原来供销社的业务。由于个体经营模式比较灵活,因此个体药店在宁波发展得很好。但是,个体药店增多最终导致市场出现了恶性竞争,行业利润空间被严重压缩。如果一个药店的某种药品降价,那么几乎宁波所有的个体药店都会跟随。比如,感冒灵颗粒进价是8.5元,在正常的竞争环境下,零售价会在进价的基础上上浮10%～15%,即零售价为9.35～9.78元。但是宁波的个体药店可能会打折到4.8元,每销售一盒就会亏损3.7元。这是因为宁波的个体药店大多采用的是通过部分低价单品吸引消费者进店,然后引导消费者购买其他高价产品的经营方式。随着竞争加剧,为了吸引消费者,越来越多的产品以低价销售,利润越来越少。严重下滑的利润使得原有的目标任务难以实现,原有的店长承包模式激励效果显著下降。

(2) 医保改革进一步压缩个体药店的生存空间

医保改革会带来药品市场增容,把定点药店纳入基本药物报销范围,实施"医药分开",长期而言对药店是利好的。但是并非所有患者都会凭处方到零售药店购买药物。同时,由于基层医疗机构的药房可以在政府补贴下以"零差率"销售基本药物,而个体药店不但拿不到政府补贴,还要缴纳租金、税费等,因此个体药店原有的价格优势不复存在。

(3) 药店连锁经营渐成趋势

由于行业的特殊性,政府对医药行业的监管非常严格。对监管部门而言,监管数量庞大的、各自为政的个体药店的成本非常高,而监管标准化运营的连锁药店则相对容易。事实上,监管部门对药店的连锁经营是持支持态度的。根据药品监督管理统计报告,截至2021年6月底,全国药店数为58.6万家,比2016年增加了13.9

万家，其中连锁药店增加了 11.5 万家。面对这样的行业趋势，小徐的药店也面临连锁改制的压力。采取连锁经营后，药店的进货权将统一交给总公司，店长不再拥有进货权。那么，原来小徐采用的店长承包模式，是否还可以有效地激励店长？如果不能有效地激励店长，那么她应该选择哪些方式进行激励？

## 【案例问题】

1. 根据马斯洛需要层次论，分析医药零售业存在的激励问题主要有哪些？

2. 请用一个或多个激励理论，解释小徐采用的店长承包模式为什么能够很好地激励店长。

3. 在新的行业变革下，原有的店长承包模式会面临什么样的挑战？应该如何激励店长？

## 【分析提示】

1. 根据马斯洛需要层次论，医药零售业的员工激励问题贯穿了不同层级的需求。如果收入不足以提供良好的生活水平，生理需求就不能满足；如果每天总是一个人长时间单独守店，社交需求就不能满足；如果职业上升空间狭窄，尊重需求就不能满足。

【目标设置理论】

2. 可以从员工激励角度展开分析，可能涉及的理论包括马斯洛需要层次论、双因素理论、目标设置理论、公平理论等。

3. 应分析新的外部环境变化对企业运营的影响，并强调环境变化会迫使企业对员工激励方式做出相应调整。在本案例中，以前适用的可以激励店长的模式可能不再有效。因为在连锁经营模式下总部会标准化药店经营的每个环节，留给店长的利润空间非常有限。这时，应该考虑非货币类的激励方式。例如，给员工提供能够使其更好地平衡生活与工作的工作方式，提供职业发展机会，提供更好的工作环境，等等。

# 案例 14

## 京博的领导实践

**【案例正文】**

山东京博控股集团有限公司（以下简称京博）是一家涉足石油化工、精细化工、现代农业等多个领域的大型民营企业。京博将中国传统儒家文化作为企业管理的本源，以为客户生产满意商品，为社会培养有益人才为使命，形成了以仁孝为核心的企业文化体系。在董事长马韵升的带领下，京博先后荣获全国重合同守信用企业、全国企业文化建设工作先进单位、中国企业500强等荣誉称号。

## 1. 仁孝文化为企业奠基

京博董事长马韵升认为企业文化是一个企业的灵魂，中国企业不能机械地搬运西方管理理念，应当基于我国的传统文化开创符合自己企业特色的管理文化。他提出经营管理要"以术悟道，以道御术"，只有用中国文化赋能企业，才能实现赶超。为此，马韵升致力于"产业发展与社会型企业构建、中国传统文化应用与企业管理"研究，坚持将国学文化作为企业管理的本源，建立了以仁孝为核心的企业文化体系，他致力于把京博做成对社会更负责、更有益的企业，创建具有东方智慧的管理文化。

## 2. 利他成就企业

从儒家的角度来看，经营是一种掌握人心理的过程，只有"动之以情"才会得到好的管理效果。在此基础上，马韵升提炼出"研究人性、经营人心、管理行为、控制风险、满足需求"的经营管理之道。这就要求管理者以仁爱之心对待员工，用真诚的情感与员工进行心灵上的沟通。要达到"仁"，就要懂得"忠恕之道"，为他人着想是"忠"，对待他人宽厚是"恕"。因此，经营企业就是经营自己的良心，利他才能成就自己。

京博从传统文化中汲取智慧，注重与员工之间达成心灵契约，这样员工管理就能够依靠员工个人的道德水平和自律精神来实现。例如，京博的各类报销全凭信任。

不论是普通员工还是各级主管,都只需在企业内网提交报销申请,无须任何领导签字,就可以拿着票据去财务部门领取款项,报销时唯一需要做的就是对着宣誓墙念一遍诚信誓言,对自己的行为做出承诺。这种对员工的与众不同的信任,旨在激励和培养员工的诚实品德,员工在感受到被信任的同时也会以真诚的态度回报企业。员工和企业的良性互动,极大地提高了报销效率。

马韵升常说,京博是属于所有对京博有感情的员工的家族企业,而不是他自己的家族企业。在京博,所有的员工都是一家人,而家人的健康对马韵升来说是至关重要的。由于常年坐着办公,又整日应酬不断,亚健康逐渐成为困扰很多成年人的问题。在京博,本着对家人的关怀,京博每季度都会为员工提供体检。此外,京博还施行了"禁酒令",工作日全面禁酒。有一次,马韵升在应酬时推脱不下,喝了酒,他上班后做的第一件事就是主动向全体员工认错,并自罚30万元现金。一杯酒,30万元,自此"禁酒令"就在京博全面贯彻落实下去。不少京博人说,他们以前陪客户,酒局很多,全面禁酒后,在家的时间多了,家庭关系更加和睦融洽,还经常有时间参加各种文体活动,身体状态也有了明显改善。京博的这些规定和要求不仅是员工对企业的责任与承诺,更是企业对每一位员工的关怀与责任。

**3. 爱父母、爱企业、爱国家**

在京博发展过程中,马韵升将"小孝治家、中孝治企、大孝治国"理念融入京博,在国内民营企业中首创"孝工资"制度,树牢尊老敬老的良好风气。从2007年开始,京博对全体员工的父母发放"孝工资";为员工年龄超过70周岁的父母每月发放敬老金,为了使孝文化更好地落地,京博与博兴县农村合作银行联合制作了"泰山·京博孝文化卡"。该联名卡是以员工父母的姓名办理的银行借记卡,用于"孝工资"的存取。京博符合条件的员工的父母每月都会收到"孝工资"。此外,京博从2014年开始对进入企业20年及以上的员工的父母每人每月发放"忠孝敬老金",以嘉奖一直以来和企业一起奋斗的员工。马韵升认为,发钱不是目的而是手段,企业替员工表孝心,不只是想对员工家属表达感恩之情,更是想为员工创造一个工作时间之外的身心愉悦的生活环境。为此,京博将仁孝文化注入企业的血液,培养员工爱父母、爱企业、爱国家的价值观，马韵升认为只要京博的文化不出问题，京博就不会出问题。京博致力于提高每位员工的社会责任感与担当意识，打造一支有爱心、敢承担、知廉耻、不忘回报社会的队伍。

**4. 尾声**

成功创业的企业家不少，但是像马韵升这样将企业文化打造为金字招牌的企业家却屈指可数。仁孝京博这4个字不仅是中华优秀传统文化的缩影，而且彰显了企业家的智慧。京博秉承"产业报国、服务社会"的理念，将东方文化智慧和西方管理实践相结合，形成了具有中国智慧的管理模式，同时也为员工打造了一个温暖的家园，在企业发展方面走出一条独特而引人深思的成功之路。

【案例问题】

1. 根据案例内容，分析领导者的作用是什么。
2. 根据当代"魅力型－愿景型领导"理论，分析马韵升的领导方式。
3. 根据赫茨伯格的双因素理论，分析马韵升是如何调动员工工作积极性的。

【分析提示】

1. 首先，一个优秀的领导者要确定好企业的发展方向，分辨出哪些是正确的事情并且知道什么时候安排谁去做，如案例中马韵升以仁孝文化奠定企业"小孝治家、中孝治企、大孝治国"的发展理念。其次，领导者要制定企业的规则，企业倡导什么、反对什么都要由具体的规章制度来体现。值得注意的是，员工会把领导者当作榜样，因此领导者要以身作则，如案例中马韵升为了推行禁酒文化以身作则。最后，领导者要激励员工，争取员工的信任与合作，使员工更有效率地完成工作，如案例中马韵升关心员工健康、为员工父母发放工资，在获得员工爱戴的同时也极大地促进了工作效率的提升。

2. 魅力型领导者是指热情、自信，人格魅力和行动能够影响他人，以某些特定方式行事的领导者。愿景型领导者能够创造并清晰传达一个可行、可信、吸引人、可以改善当前状况的未来愿景（该愿景如果能正确地界定和实施，将具有很强的感染力和激励作用），并通过聚集各方的技能、才干和资源使其成为现实。在本案例中，马韵升以身作则，在企业内部推崇仁孝文化，以利他的形式对待员工，并且注意培养员工诚实、担当的品格。员工认可马韵升的领导方式，因而公司内部凝聚力极强，这种领导方式有助于促进企业绩效增长。

3.根据双因素理论可知，内在激励因素与工作满意状态相关，而外在保健因素与工作不满意状态相关。赫茨伯格认为，保健因素和激励因素相互独立，并且差异很大。保健因素只能安抚员工，没有激励作用，不能使员工产生工作满意感。激励因素会使员工感受到内部的回报，对员工具有激励作用。因此，要想真正激励员工努力工作，就必须注重激励因素，只有这些内在激励因素才能提高员工的工作满意度。在本案例中，员工在工作中被给予了充分的信任，如报销不需要签字，认可员工的贡献并为员工父母发放"孝工资"，倡导京博是全体员工的家族企业而不是董事长个人的家族企业等。这些激励使得员工对工作具有很高的满意度，因此他们的工作效率也很高。

【双因素理论】

## 案例 15

### 捷丰的控制管理

## 【案例正文】

捷丰是一家制造和销售以不锈钢和木材为主要原料的厨浴家居用品的公司。捷丰拥有强大的生产制造、成本控制和设计开发能力，已建立并完善了"质量管理体系"和"社会责任体系"。捷丰每年约有86%的产品以代工方式提供给宜家，是宜家在中国华东地区的不锈钢家居产品生产基地，也是其在亚洲屈指可数的明星供应商。捷丰的业绩与其良好的控制机制密不可分。

**1. 权力制衡控风险**

捷丰由鲍氏家族和香港合作者联合控股，其中香港合作者持有55%的股份，不涉及日常管理，仅参与重大决策；鲍氏家族持有45%的股份，由家族第二代管理者鲍向前负责日常管理。这一独特的治理模式与鲍向前的经历有关。鲍向前具有较强的创业激情和能力，但风险控制意识不足。而香港合作者是一位公认的"理性商人"，在财务决策和风险控制上具有丰富经验，并且认可鲍向前的管理能力，适合作为外部力量约束家族管理者的冒险行为。

选择能力互补的合作者，稀释股权降低决策风险，是鲍父在反复思考后做出的重要决定。为此，鲍氏家族将55%的股份转让给香港合作者，仅保留45%的股份和企业管理权。这一股权设置的优势在于，每年公司的年终报告和重大计划都须交由股东会议审议，香港合作者可以对管理层提出意见和建议，并对关键事项具有一票否决权。以鲍向前为代表的家族管理层全权负责日常管理，监控、比较和纠正工作绩效，以完成计划并实施控制。这种混合结构使投资方和管理方之间形成了一种制约关系，可以避免管理方作出冒进决策。

**2. 直面困难干中学**

1998年，鲍父创立捷丰不锈钢公司，承接本地钣金业务。1999年，鲍向前带来了宜家10万个不锈钢垃圾桶订单，这份订单远超鲍父预想。想成为宜家的供应商必须能够提供高质量、低成本的产品，而捷丰当时的工厂只有500平方米，生产实力有限，无论是技术还是场地，都很难达到要求。同时，根据宜家的报价，鲍父认为工厂难以实现盈亏平衡，因此极力反对接单。但鲍向前却认为，宜家是个好客户，即使这份订单不赚钱，后续也可能会带来稳定的大订单。最终鲍向前说服父亲接下了订单，鲍氏父子与宜家的合作正式启动。恰逢该年经济环境波动导致原材料成本下降，因此这笔订单并未亏损。此后，随着宜家的新订单陆续到来，鲍向前的能力也得到了鲍父和香港合作者的认可，他正式进入捷丰的核心管理层成为联合创始人。

2005年，宜家原有的订单已不能满足捷丰刚刚上市需要快速发展的需要，因此捷丰主动提出想为宜家生产供应本土的木制家具。宜家没有否决这一提议，但提出捷丰需在三个月内对一个产品系列进行打样，并与其他三家工厂竞争供应商的资格。捷丰立刻组织团队，斥资购买了全套设备和原材料，在狭小的场地完成从研发到生产的全套流程，自主设计并完成了样品。宜家的竞标在上海举行，捷丰虽然产品水平高于其他工厂，但是资质不足。为改变劣势，鲍向前提出了匿名评审的做法，建议宜家高管对样品进行盲选。最终，捷丰在盲选中获得4票，成功中标。自此，捷丰拿下了宜家的木制家具订单，新增订单与上市融资催生了捷丰的跨越式发展，短短一年，捷丰从一家不锈钢厂扩建为兼顾木制家具生产的标准化工厂。

2007年，随着捷丰成本控制能力的大幅度提高，拿下代表宜家家具最高技术水平的蜂窝板家具业务成为捷丰的战略目标，蜂窝板家具是以往只有宜家全资子公司才有资格生产的产品。为了拿下该业务，捷丰针对技术差异调整控制方法，大力投入技术研发，开发出贴纸替代油漆、缩短冷压时间、桌子桌腿密封包装、木制框设计四项突破性技术，通过流程控制大幅度降低了原有蜂窝板家具的成本。这些突破获得了宜家的肯定，由此捷丰拿下了宜家的蜂窝板家具订单，并在整个宜家供应商体系里占据了独一无二的地位。

### 3. 精益控制创佳绩

捷丰在技术创新上不断寻求突破，在控制管理上不断进行精简，以促进绩效增长。一方面，技术创新成本最低，带来的利润增长空间却非常大，被认为是最佳的绩效增长途径。精益是捷丰从与宜家多年的合作经验中归纳出的技术与管理理念。在此理念下，捷丰的技术人员在产品设计和开发方面，力求简约和高质并存，比如具有捷丰特色的蜂窝板家具技术，正是在流程控制和技术革新上追求极致的结果。

另一方面，捷丰基于绩效增长设置了"超产和质量奖"，通过调整绩效来控制员工行为，这也是捷丰目前唯一采取的绩效管理措施。例如，"超产和质量奖"是在确保质量的情况下，由财务经理基于现有的产品结构计算出公司的盈亏平衡点，将基于该盈亏平衡点计算出的销售量作为"超产和质量奖"起点，把每个月扣除公司固定开销后的超产部分的销售额按比例折算成奖金下发给员工。但是如果某部门出现问题影响了当月产量，那么当月全部员工的超产奖金可能都会被取消。每过三年，财务经理会重新计算盈亏平衡点。对于各部门应占的权重，公司会充分考虑各部门的意见，确保公正客观，避免员工产生不公平感。在这种绩效管理模式下，由于产量与自身利益挂钩，因此每个员工都非常关心公司每个月的生产情况，各部门之间互相监督，朝着绩效增长的共同目标而努力，每年公司的人才流失率只有5%左右。

鲍向前认为，最好的控制就是设置一个"干净"的运营模式，制订简单至极的规则，让员工没有争议的空间，从而将主要的精力集中到生产本身，自觉思考自己的行为与实际绩效的关系，并调整自己的行为以实现最终目标。在创业过程中，鲍向前总是观察其他管理体系中最有价值的部分，将其吸纳到自己的企业中，用最少的资源做最想要做的事情，用精益思路持续创新，用治理结构严控风险。

## 【案例问题】

1. 捷丰采用了哪些控制措施？取得了什么样的成效？请结合案例分析控制对组织的重要性。

2. 以捷丰为例，分析企业为了实现财务控制，需要如何调整组织结构。

3. 请结合案例内容，分析捷丰是如何对组织绩效进行控制的？

## 【分析提示】

【控制为什么重要?】

1. 控制是指管理者测量实际绩效,将实际绩效与标准绩效进行比较,并对偏差进行纠正。控制的重要性在于:①它是管理者了解目标是否实现以及目标为何没有实现的唯一方法;②它能够提供必要的信息和反馈,从而使管理者放心地实施员工授权;③它能帮助保护组织及资产。控制的标准是管理者在计划过程中设定的目标。从本案例可以看出,捷丰聚焦于超产和保证质量两个目标,它围绕这两个目标设定相应的标准,引导员工自主完成目标。可以从如何设置管理目标来理解控制的意义和控制的标准。主要涉及的知识点有控制的定义、性质和重要性。

2. 当代的控制问题需要考虑特定的情境,我们可以以控制绩效为目标进行独特的家族企业组织结构设计。捷丰为了避免决策失误,以家族和外部财务投资者共治的方式实施财务控制,如通过审议财务报告、设置财务测量标准来降低关键决策风险。主要涉及的知识点有财务控制和组织结构。

3. 管理者需要合适的工具来监控和测量组织绩效,组织绩效是组织中所有工作活动的累积结果。组织绩效的三种常用测量标准包括:①生产率,即产品或服务的总产出与产生这些产出的总投入的比值;②组织效力,它是对组织目标的合适程度以及实现程度的测量;③由各种商业出版物公布的公司排名。在本案例中,可以从捷丰设置的"超产和质量奖"来理解如何测量组织绩效,进而控制员工行为。主要涉及的知识点有组织绩效和生产率。

# Case 1

## Management Key of Sunny

## *Case Description*

Sunny Optical Technology Co., Ltd. (hereinafter referred to as Sunny) was founded in 1984 in Yuyao, Zhejiang Province, and has become a leading global manufacturer of integrated optical components and products. It was listed on the main board of the Hong Kong Stock Exchange in June 2007. Sunny specializes in the design, R&D, production and sales of optical and optoelectronic related products. The main products include three categories: First, optical components, mainly including glass/plastic lenses, mobile phone lenses, automotive lenses, security surveillance lenses and various other lenses; Second, optoelectronic products, mainly including mobile phone camera modules, 3D optoelectronic modules, automotive modules and other optoelectronic modules; Third, optical instruments, mainly including microscopes and intelligent detection equipment. Currently, Sunny has formed eight business sectors: mobile phones, automobiles, security, micro instruments, robotics, AR/VR, industrial testing, and medical testing.

From a company with no capital, no people and no technology, it has developed into a star in the optoelectronic industry today. Sunny's growth could not be achieved without the leadership of its founder Wang Wenjian. Wang Wenjian believes that if a company would like to win in the fierce market competition, the management must make correct decisions on the company's production and operation in a timely manner based on changes in internal and external environmental conditions. In the face of changes in the market environment or unexpected events, the management must execute timely control, and find corresponding solutions, only in this way can the enterprise achieve success.

**1. The Start of Optical Component Processing**

In 1983, in order to cultivate excellent technical backbone, technical personnel, the Chengbei Commune of Yuyao signed an agreement with the Optical Instrument Factory of Zhejiang University to send personnel to the latter to study the optical cold processing technique. The team was led by Wang Wenjian, quality inspector of Yuyao Capacitor Electric Appliance Factory then. In November 1984, Wang Wenjian, who returned from training, led 8 high school graduates and obtained a loan of RMB 60,000 to establish the predecessor of Sunny, Yuyao No.2 Optical Instrument Factory (hereinafter referred to as Optical Instrument Factory). As the optical industry across China was in a downturn, the previously agreed orders from the Optical Instrument Factory of Zhejiang University was canceled. Whether or not to obtain processing orders become the primary issue for the survival of the newly established optical instrument factory. At this critical moment, based on the effective information provided by the Hangzhou Photographic Machinery Research Institute of the Ministry of Machinery, Wang Wenjian predicted that the camera would become a best-selling product with the improvement of people's living standard. The production of optical components of the camera lenses were not only suitable for the newly established optical instrument factory, but also provided a rare opportunity for Sunny to start the production of camera lenses. As such, Wang Wenjian set the goal of entering the field of camera lenses production. As a result, the factory started to produce Haiyan I camera lens for Zhejiang Camera No. 1 Factory. In retrospect, this decision was successful. If not, Sunny might still be lingering amidst difficulties.

## 2. Expand Production through Horizontal Strategic Partnerships

In the second half of 1986, after careful discussions with the management, Wang Wenjian decided to implement lateral strategic partnership plan with a major camera manufacturer to strengthen its own capabilities, thereby enabling the company to develop rapidly. Wang Wenjian believed that, on the one hand, the technical quality of employees had been greatly improved through several years of education and training, and the production capacity had been continuously expanded; while on the other hand, the sales of Zhejiang Camera No. 1 Factory, the main client at the time, was experiencing a decline in sales, which once again put Sunny's production in crisis. The situation forced the company to seek new opportunities. In the market research process, director Li Kang, an old friend from the Hangzhou Photographic Machinery Research Institute, brought an important message to Wang Wenjian: Tianjin Camera Factory planned to expand production and intended to find lenses producers across China. This was a great opportunity. Therefore, Wang Wenjian seized the opportunity and immediately expressed his desire to produce Dongfang S4 camera lenses for Tianjin Camera Company. Since Sunny was still in start-up phase and not well-known, it was difficult to establish cooperation with top domestic camera companies at that time. In preparation for site inspection by Tianjin Camera Company, Wang Wenjian did a good job with his team and invited leaders of Yuyao government for support, fully showing the company's determination and sincerity in this cooperation. In the end, the representative of Tianjin Camera Company was moved by the "Four Thousand" spirit of the team led by Wang Wenjian, and promised to give Sunny a chance. "Four Thousand" spirit refers to "Traveling through mountains and rivers, Speaking thousands of words, Trying every means, and Enduring countless hardships". As a test, Sunny had to deliver 1000 sets of qualified lenses within only 75 days. At that time, Sunny was also facing competition with a long-established military industry company in Nanjing and Shanghai Nanhui Optical Instrument Factory. Wang Wenjian was under tremendous pressure.

To complete this task, Wang Wenjian relied on his existing contacts to use the bakelite factory's warehouse as the company's production workshop and hired an experienced technician from Jiangxi Optical Instrument factory to conduct sample trial production research with new processes. To meet the product processing requirements, Wang Wenjian decided to purchase a second-hand fine grinding and polishing equipment from a Japanese company that had ceased production in Beijing. The equipment was installed and tested overnight after delivery. In addition, Wang Wenjian carried out a precise division of labor for each department and encouraged all employees to be confident in completing this task. After more than 70 days of hard work, Sunny completed the production of 1000 sets of samples on time. For the sake of quality, Wang Wenjian also invited professionals to conduct a careful and detailed inspection of the 1000 sets of samples. In the end, all the samples were qualified and delivered to Tianjin Camera Company within the agreed timeline. At this time, the other two competitors had not yet completed the work.

In 1987, the "Agreement on Strategic Cooperation between Tianjin Camera Company and Yuyao No.2 Optical Instrument Factory" was signed, making the position of Sunny changed from the original general processing to strategic supply. In order to further improve production efficiency, Sunny introduced key national scientific research results for technological transformation. That greatly improved Sunny's processing technique capabilities. Furthermore, Sunny also obtained advanced production techniques from Tianjin Camera Company. Sunny's production efficiency far exceeded that of many domestic large factories at that time. In just one year of strategic cooperation, these measures had paid off. The company's output value increased from RMB 512,900 to RMB 3,213,600, and profits increased from RMB 131,400 to RMB 463,400. The annual production orders from Tianjin Camera Company have increased to 100,000 sets.

### 3. Enter the International Market

In the 1990s, with the continuous development of science and technology, optical technology was demanded and applied by more industries. In the optical industry, the number of manufacturers continued to increase and competition in the domestic optical market was becoming increasingly fierce. At the same time, the international market's demand for low and medium lenses and lens glass is increasing day by day.

Along with this idea, Wang Wenjian proposed the strategy of "two transformations" in the second half of 1988: From only domestic market to both domestic market and international market; From only component processing to both component processing and complete equipment production. But at that time, foreign companies had high requirements for product quality but offered low prices, and more importantly, they held the initiative in negotiations and could cancel deals at will, leaving the manufacturers to bear the risk of failed transactions.

For Sunny, the previous "production merely according to drawings" obviously could not meet the demand of international market. Sunny must carry out the design based on the technical parameters provided by foreign clients. It was unrealistic for Sunny to train employees to a satisfactory level within a short period of time. However, if it could cooperate with Zhejiang University and rely on Zhejiang University's research and development capabilities, the products could quickly enter the international market. For Zhejiang University, having good techniques but not the production capacity is also a problem. Soon Sunny and Zhejiang University Optoelectronics Technology Development Company formed a scientific and technological production consortium, relying on the "Zhejiang University design, Sunny production" model for cooperative production. With the deepening of joint production and the need to establish a modern enterprise system, the consortium was reorganized into Zhejiang University Yuyao Optoelectronics (Group) Co., Ltd. in 1994.

After that, Sunny's market has expanded to the United States, Canada, etc. For example, POC, a US company, had an increasing demand for various lenses and optical components produced by Sunny.

## 4. The Success of the Great Supporting Role Strategy

In 2003, Wang Wenjian carefully analyzed the domestic and international macroeconomic changes and the current situation of Sunny's development and formally proposed the "Great Supporting Role Strategy": First, serve the "leading role" who refers to a well-known company in the international optoelectronic industry, with global influence and popularity, the "supporting role" and the "leading role" form a strategic partnership; Second, the "supporting role" itself must have high reputation and goodwill, as well as influence on a global scale.

Wang Wenjian believed that the future development direction of the mobile phone camera modules would be towards high-resolution and the existing (Chip Scale Package) process cannot keep up with the future trend. He set up teams in advance to purchase relevant equipment and prepare for the establishment of COB (Chips on Board) production line.

From the perspective of market applications, CSP packaging is mainly used in areas below 8 million pixels, and COB can be used in areas above 8 million pixels but requires higher investment in equipment. After the COB production line was put into service, the high-resolution market stagnated for a while, and it was not until 2010 that the high pixel market started to boost. As a result, Sunny has been able to realize corner overtaking and cut into the supply chain of most well-known mobile phone manufacturers, becoming the leading supplier in the smartphone field.

After years of implementation, the "Great Supporting Role Strategy" has shown great power. It has not only brought Sunny's development back on the track of rapid growth, but also maintained it. The company's sales revenue has increased from 2004's RMB 400 million to RMB 38 billion in 2020, representing an increase of nearly 94 times.

Looking back at Sunny's development history, it can be found that from the initial camera lens processing to complex optical instruments production, to today's sophisticated mobile phone camera modules, the founder Wang Wenjian always made the right decisions at critical moments, successfully leading Sunny from an unfamous township enterprise to a world leading manufacturer of integrated optical products.

## Questions

1. With the development of Sunny, how has the management role of founder Wang Wenjian changed?

2. At different stages of Sunny's development, what management skills did the founder Wang Wenjian exhibit? How did he effectively perform management functions?

## Tips for Answering the Questions

1. Based on the changes in the decision made by Wang Wenjian during Sunny's develop-

ment, use the management role theory to analyze the manager's role in the organization.

2. Based on Wang Wenjian's solution to the difficult problems faced by Sunny during its development, apply management skill theory and management function theory to explain how the skills of managers change as the company develops, and how managers execute the four major management functions of planning, organizing, leading, and controlling.

【What Do Managers Do?】

# Case 2

## Corporate Culture of Novel Optics

## Case Description

Novel Optics was founded in 1997 and is located in Ningbo High-tech Zone, Zhejiang Province. It is an optical enterprise specializing in the production of microscopes and optical components. With independent brands such as NOVEL, NEXCOPE, Jiangnan and an annual production output of more than 100000 optical microscopes and tens of millions of optical components, it is the core supplier of internationally renowned companies such as Leica, Zeiss and Nikon, etc. In 2017, Novel Optics was selected by Ministry of Industry and Information Technology as National Manufacturing Single Champion Cultivation Enterprise for its optical microscope products. In 2019, ISO 9345-2019 Microscopes—Interfacing dimensions for imaging components with Novel Optics as the leading sponsor was published. In the same year, Novel Optics won the Second Prize of National Technological Invention. In 2021, it successfully passed the reevaluation and was upgraded to National Manufacturing Single Champion Demonstration Enterprise.

Novel Optics' ability to evolve from initially producing low-end microscope to manufacturing a variety of optical lenses for Chang'e satellites and from a enterprise that only processed elementary components to a leading enterprise in the optical microscope industry, is rooted in its core values of "Honesty, Perfection, Truthfulness and Innovation". Since the beginning of its establishment, the corporate culture of Novel Optics has inspired every employee of the company.

### 1. The Establishment of Novel Optics

Mr. Cao Guangbiao, with ancestral home at Ningbo, is a well-known entrepreneur in China, and a representative figure of the overseas Ningbo business circle. He is known as the "King of Woolen Textile". With the aspiration to rejuvenate the country through science and education, Cao invested in Ningbo Optical Instrument Factory in 1997 and then completed the restructuring into Ningbo Novel Optics Co., Ltd. In Cao's mind, the roadmap to a strong country is the development of its key instruments, which has also become the unremitting pursuit of Novel Optics.

In 1997, Zhejiang University celebrated its 100th anniversary. Cao attended the celebration and asked the professors of the Department of Optics of Zhejiang University to assist in finding a manager who understood technology and had an international view to manage Novel Optics. At that time, several professors of the Department of Optics recommended Mao Lei. Cao's personal charm and expectations for the future development of China Optical impressed Mao Lei and built up his confidence in the company's business in the near future. Mao Lei immediately decided to accept this challenge and was appointed as the General Manager and Chief Engineer of Novel Optics.

When handing over the management control of the company to Mao Lei, Cao only stated one principle: no matter how the reform was done, no employee should be laid off, and they should be treated well. In 1997, Novel Optics faced many challenges, such as single product structure, low quality, a large number of old and retired employees, and strikes due to labor disputes. The management had discussions and agreed that no employee would be fired, but the company would only have room for survival by developing relatively profitable mid-to-high-end biological microscopes and optical components, and by selling the products to developed countries such as Europe and the United States. At that time, it happened that the purchasing director of Motorola came to China to seek a cooperative manufacturer of optical laser pick-up lens and contacted Novel Optics. Novel Optics took it seriously. Based on the client's requirements for product processing, all the technical engineers of the factory worked overnights in cooperation for product and process design and finally designed a satisfactory solution for Motorola. The two parties immediately signed a contract worth multi-million RMB. This cooperation helped Novel Optics to pull through the crisis.

Subsequently, Novel Optics strengthened its cooperation with leading companies in the industry. After establishing a partnership with Motorola, it began to cooperate with international leading companies such as Nikon and Leica. As microscopes and optical components have the characteristics of high precision, multi-variety and small batch, the main form of cooperation was "production based on sales", i.e., to provide product manufacturing process plans according to customer needs and conduct processing. Novel Optics maintained close contact with customers under such cooperative model, and the number of orders increased year by year. The company acquired sufficient funds and also achieved a steady improvement in the production process.

**2. University-Industry Collaboration**

In 2010, the Chang'e-2 satellite was successfully launched into space. The surveillance camera lens on the satellite was jointly developed by Novel Optics and Zhejiang University over a period of five years. The lens was required to withstand the acceleration of the rocket during take-off and the harsh external environment of the moon surface while ensuring photo taking function. It was of extremely high quality. The development of the surveillance lens not only improved the R&D capabilities of Novel Optics, but also enhanced the corporate social responsibility and mission. In 2013, Novel Optics once again teamed up with Zhejiang University to develop a landing camera lens for Chang'e-3.

The successful development of Chang'e-2 camera lens and Chang'e-3 camera lens has expanded the breadth and depth of cooperation between Novel Optics and major universities. For example, Novel Optics established collaboration with Tsinghua University, Ningbo University and other universities, signed the Master Degree Postgraduate Joint Training Agreement with Zhejiang University and jointly built post-doctoral workstations to train the scientific research personnel and comprehensive talents needed by the company. In 2016, Novel Optics, Zhejiang University, University of Shanghai for Science and Technology, Fudan University Affiliated Hospital and Nanjing Medical University jointly undertook the national major scientific instrument development project Research and Industrialization of High-resolution Fluorescence Microscopic Imager, which was one of the most beneficial projects in the university-industry collaboration of Novel Optics. The high-resolution fluorescence microscopy imager adopted large numerical aperture objective lens imaging, differential interference technology and digital image display technology, which can be used in four-dimensional automatic analysis and measurement. It could be applied in the fields of oncology, immunology and cell biology, which had good market prospects and formed a solid foundation for Novel Optics to further enter the high-end microscope market.

university-Industry collaboration has greatly improved the technological leadership and quality reliability of the products developed by Novel Optics. After the enhancement in domestic recognition, Novel Optics had greater confidence to work with manufacturers in international market.

### 3. Continuous Innovation

In 2018, Novel Optics was successfully listed on the Shanghai Stock Exchange. After the listing, Novel Optics has increased its investment in product research and development. In 2019, the "Super-resolution Optical Micro-Nano Microscopy Imaging Technology" jointly declared by Novel Optics and Zhejiang University won the second prize of National Technology Invention. This technology broke through optical diffraction limit, solved the problem of foreign super-resolution optical imaging limited by special dyes and narrow adaptation range, and provided effective technical support for the fields of cranial nerves, life sciences, nano-pharmaceuticals, etc. In 2019, Novel Optics worked with Zhejiang University, Ningbo "Five-in-One" Campus Education Development Center and Zhejiang University Optoelectronics College to jointly establish the Optoelectronics Branch of Ningbo Research Institute of Zhejiang University, creating a deep university-industry integration. Featuring Novel Optics as the main body, and oriented by industry-leading technology, it aggregated the R&D capabilities of universities and research institutes, and has laid a solid foundation for Novel Optics to assume a role in major national scientific research projects.

In 2019, the camera lens that captured the first image of the Chang'e-4 landing on the moon came from Novel Optics. This lens not only enabled Chang'e-4 to take pictures of the rugged surface of the moon, but also assisted Chang'e-4 to avoid dangerous areas and choose the safest spot when landing. For this lens, the R&D team of Novel Optics worked very hard, made trial and error for more than a hundred lenses and accumulated tens of thousands of sets of data.

Relying on the key scientific research project of the Ministry of Science and Technology—Automated Scanning and Analysis System Development, Novel Optics was engaged in research on large-field high-resolution microscopic images and high-throughput computer-aided rapid detection, and further expanded the embedded microscope system business to life sciences and biomedical sciences. The company gradually launched products such as fiber analyzers and blood cell morphology analyzers. On April 29, 2021, the Long March-5B Y2 rocket of China, carrying the Tianhe module, blasted off from the Wenchang Spacecraft Launch Site. Together with Tianhe was China's first space fluorescence microscopy experimental device developed by Novel Optics, assisting the astronauts to carry out research on space medicine and space life science and biotechnology.

From installing "Celestial Eyes" on satellite Chang'e-2 in 2010, and subsequently on Chang'e-3, and Chang'e-4, to manufacturing China's first space fluorescence microscopy experimental device in 2020, Novel Optics has continuously participated in China's aerospace industry. All the achievements couldn't have been made without the corporate culture of Novel Optics who holds the vision of "becoming a trusted and respected global enterprise and establishing a high-quality image of Chinese scientific instrument products in the world", and the mission of "continuously providing effective optical solutions for the human cognition world, and realizing the continuous improvement of the multi-party value of customers, employees, shareholders and society".

## Questions

1. How was the corporate culture of Novel Optics formed?

2. How does Novel Optics' core value of "Honesty, Perfection, Truthfulness and Innovation" affect management decision-making?

## Tips for Answering the Questions

1. The formation of Novel Optics' corporate culture was influenced by a series of decisions and actions of the founder and its senior management. The initial source of corporate culture reflects the vision of the founder. The corporate culture is maintained and continued through the selection behavior of employees, actions of senior management and socialization processes.

【Culture and Strong Culture】

2. In an organization with a strong culture, employees are more loyal, and their performance tends to be better. The stronger the corporate culture becomes, the greater the impact it has on the way managers plan, organize, lead and control. The above knowledge points can be used to analyze the impact of Novel Optics' core values on the decision-making and behavior of senior managers.

# Case 3

## SHUYILINK Empowers the Manufacturing Industry's Digital Transformation

## Case Description

SHUYILINK is a company committed to offering "data stream + value stream" based digital software for the discrete manufacturing industry. Relying on the new generation of Internet of Things technologies, real-time interaction means and the lean thinking in industrial engineering, SHUYILINK provides end-to-end factory-level digital upgrade solutions from planning to implementation for customers of the discrete manufacturing industry. The company focuses on building an industrial data platform for the manufacturing industry, and consistently providing data intelligence service for the customers.

SHUYILINK was founded in June 2020. As a young and vigorous company, it has attracted venture capital investment from several well-known venture capital firms including China Growth Capital, GL Ventures and Genesis Capital. As of 2022, the company had more than one hundred employees and its estimated value exceeded RMB 500 million.

### 1. The Emergence of the Industrial Internet

Industrial Internet was first put forward by GE in 2012. In 2013, GE launched the Predix, an industrial cloud platform based on PaaS (Platform as a Service), which began the prologue for the development of international Industrial Internet cloud platform. Then in 2014, GE and other players including AT&T, Cisco, IBM, and Intel formed the Industrial Internet Consortium, which represented the preliminary ecology of the industry. Since then, the United States began to reshape the manufacturing industry in a "from top to bottom" way by leveraging the advantages of the information technology including Internet, information communication, and software.

In response to the challenges brought by the flourishing new sci-tech revolution and industrial transformation, Germany paid greater attention to its strengths in manufacturing equipment, automation system, and technological process. It proposed the Industry 4.0

strategy to reinvent its manufacturing industry in a "from bottom to top" way. In essence, the Industry 4.0 strategy was intended to interconnect the "real" world consisting of production machinery with the "virtual" world based on Internet and build a new production and manufacturing service system based on Industrial Internet to improve the efficiency of resource allocation. The Industrial Internet became a global development trend. UK and France worked out new industrial strategies to enhance support to the development of Industrial Internet in terms of technological breakthrough, industrial layout, and financial services. Japan put forward the Connected Industries strategy to interconnect personnel, equipment, systems, and technologies to create new added value and solve the related social issues. Korea took robots, artificial intelligence, automated driving, and 3D printing as the main development directions of intelligent manufacturing industry.

In China, the Industrial Internet enterprises began to emerge from 2015 when the State Council issued the "Made in China 2025" program in which the manufacturing quality power strategy was proposed for the first time. Subsequently, in 2019, the Ministry of Industry and Information Technology issued the 512 Program Proposal for Promoting "5G + Industrial Internet" to promote the upgrade of Industrial Internet further. In recent years, the Industrial Internet industry in China has made remarkable achievements. In terms of scale, the Alliance of Industrial Internet was established under the guidance of the Ministry of Industry and Information Technology and the number of members has exceeded 2000. In terms of services and products, an integrated platform service system featuring coordinated development of core layer and application layer has taken shape. The core layer platform market is highly centralized and monopolistic, while the application platform market is a less centralized market that features diversified and free development.

### 2. SHUYILINK Steams Ahead

Since the Industrial Internet concept emerged, many Internet companies and manufacturing companies in China has set their sights on the Industrial Internet market. Huawei and Alibaba built universal basic platforms and cloud service platforms. Haier launched COS-

MOPlat adapted to the transformation and upgrading demands of traditional manufacturing industry. Kingdee and Inspur created lightweight industrial Apps that could help small and medium-sized enterprises in the basic transformation towards digital, IT and automation application. XCMG and Rootcloud offered operation services for Industrial Internet platforms. Although the participation of these companies have contributed to the breakthrough of some core technologies, the SaaS (Software as a Service) technologies that can truly represent the core of the Industrial Internet still needed further development.

In 2020, He Shenghua became the Deputy CEO of IKD Co., Ltd. It was ten years since he graduated from Tsinghua University. Years of experience in the manufacturing industry helped him keep keen insight into the prospect of Industrial Internet. During his service for IKD, he commenced the transformation of IKD towards Industrial Internet application. Through this transformation, digital technologies were highly integrated with all 7 factories, 30 workshops, and 2300 sets of production equipment of IKD, which greatly improved the product quality, reduced the production cost, and shortened the lead time. He realized the dream of building IKD into a digital factory. The successful experience in IKD deepened his insight into the Industrial Internet and he began to consider "building a digital transformation platform to share the resources and experiences with others".

In August 2020, He Shenghua resolutely resigned from IKD and funded SHUYILINK with his team. They will not only focus on the digital transformation of enterprise, but also exert their ideas and technologies to develop SaaS products and build the world's first highly standardized Industrial Internet platform, which was an unprecedented career. With such a platform, the SaaS providers could provide all the network infrastructure and software/hardware operation platforms necessary for IT application of the customers and render a series of services covering frontend implementation and follow-up maintenance. The customers could use the information system via Internet, and need not purchase software and hardware, build a computer room, or recruit IT personnel. Just like turning on a tap to use water, the customers of the platform may lease the software services they need from the SaaS providers.

Within just two years after the founding of SHUYILINK, He Shenghua and his team successfully improved the standardization level of SaaS to 80% (cross-industry) and 90% (industry-specific). They are now moving toward a higher target of standardization. But there are still many challenges: ①It is necessary to explore which functions and standards could be achieved and which non-standard demands may be eliminated in the future; ②Unlike the Internet giants such as Alibaba and Tencent, SHUYILINK does not have strong support from a solid foundation, so it is necessary to strengthen the investment in software technology research and development.

### 3. SHUYILINK Forges ahead Hand in Hand with the Manufacturing Industry

In recent years, lots of enterprises tend to transform towards industrial digitalization and intelligence as guided by Industrial Internet and "Future Factory". Digital factory represents a global contest in which all competitors are lined up at the start. It is not only a challenge, but also a great opportunity for the manufacturing industry of China. He Shenghua states that many Chinese manufacturing enterprises occupy the world's first market share in the global segmented markets, especially the advanced manufacturing enterprises in Yangtze River Delta and Pearl River Delta regions. They purchase the most advanced equipment in the world, and apply digital software to realize highly automatic production of massive products. They represent the most comprehensive categories and the most suitable sites for the implementation of Digital Factory.

In August 2021, the Digital Factory Phase 1 project undertaken by SHUYILINK for Zhejiang Meishuo Electric Technology Co., Ltd. was established. The project involved 10 modules and 30 functions covering quality management, abnormality management, equipment management, barcode management, personnel management, warehousing and logistics management, planning and progress reporting management, process management, paperless document management, and reports management. Through fast implementation and deployment, SHUYILINK delivered the project for acceptance within just three months.

In September 2021, SHUYILINK entered into a strategic cooperation agreement with Ningbo L.K. Technology Co., Ltd. to carry out profound strategic cooperation on Digital Factory Phase 1 project of Ningbo L.K. Technology Co., Ltd. They selected the CNC workshop to implement digital transformation, and SHUYILINK completed digital benchmark transformation of the workshop within just three months.

In March 2022, the Digital Factory Phase 2 project of Ningbo L.K. Technology was commenced. Based on the functional modules in Phase 1, the project added several new modules to realize whole-process digitalization covering purchase, warehousing of raw materials, metal plate, CNC machine, accessories, assembly, delivery of finished products, and customer use.

In April 2022, the Digital Factory project undertaken by SHUYILINK for Asiaway Group was formally commenced. SHUYILINK and Asiaway Group aimed at building a benchmark, and one of the world's leading digital factories in the die-casting industry that is featured of transparent manufacturing process. Through this project, Asiaway Group wished that the digital transformation and upgrade could improve its comprehensive competitiveness, play the role of intelligent manufacturing and promote deep integration of the latest digital technologies with advanced manufacturing technologies to build Asiaway Group as the preferential supplier in the global automotive components industry.

By making constant optimization and upgrade of the existing products, SHUYILINK is planned to launch 100% standardized SaaS products, expand its line of products, and extend the target customers to small and medium-sized manufacturing enterprises with annual sales of over RMB 10 million.

Under the leadership of He Shenghua and his team, SHUYILINK, a young company, will be committed to building standard, highly adaptable, whole-chain, and factory-level digital solutions for the customers in the discrete manufacturing industry by relying upon their profound experience in the industry and exerting their technological advantages in Internet of Things and human-machine interaction. SHUYILINK will help Chinese manufacturers reduce cost and improve efficiency, increase the digital level of Chinese manufacturing industry, and make a contribution to high-quality development of manufacturing in China.

## Questions

1. Which external trends are confronted by the management of SHUYILINK? How will these trends influence the decisions of the management of SHUYILINK?

2. Which enterprises are the important stakeholders of SHUYILINK? What interest do these stakeholders have? Why is the stakeholder relations management so important?

## Tips for Answering the Questions

1.The case may be analyzed from the perspectives of macroeconomic environment and industry environment. Knowledge points involved in this case: macro factors such as population, globalization, and political, economic, social, technical factors; industrial factors such as supplier, purchaser, substitute, potential industrial player, and internal competition of industry.

【How the Environment Affects Managers?】

2. The case may be analyzed from the perspective of stakeholder management and may involve the following knowledge points. The stakeholders include employees, consumers, shareholders, suppliers, competitors, communities, and governments. Their interests vary and might conflict with each other. Through the stakeholder relations management, the enterprise may better predict the changes in external environment, make innovations more successfully, build more trusty relationship with the stakeholders, and respond to the external changes more flexibly.

# Case 4

## Green Management Practices of Tsingshan

## Case Description

Tsingshan Holding Group Company Limited (hereinafter referred to as Tsingshan) is a large enterprise in heavy industry specializing in stainless steel manufacturing. Tsingshan has always put its environmental protection responsibilities as the top priority since its founding. Mr. Xiang Guangda, who founded Tsingshan and led Tsingshan to grow into a world's leading enterprise, often states that "lucid waters and lush mountains are invaluable assets." For an enterprise, if the plant and equipment are considered as the body and the leaders are considered as the brain, then the corporate culture will be just like its soul and nature. Under the leadership and influence of Xiang Guangda, the green development concept has been deeply integrated into the corporate culture of Tsingshan and kept in mind and put into practice by all employees of Tsingshan. Over the years, the green development concept was rooted in the heart of all employees of Tsingshan and practiced in the construction of every project and the daily operation and management of every factory. In particular, Tsingshan always adheres to high standards and stringent requirements and makes technological and process innovations constantly to fulfill its environmental protection responsibilities.

## 1. Innovations in Smelting Technology: Introducing the RKEF Process and Creating Duplex Process

Xiang Guangda was first introduced to the RKEF (Rotary Kiln Electric Furnace) process in March 2007 when he was negotiating with Aneka Tambang, a company in Indonesia, for purchasing nickel ore. RKEF was a highly efficient production process that integrated rotary kiln with electric furnace smelter to smelt nickel laterite into refined ferronickel. At that time, the RKEF process represented an advanced technology and had been promoted in foreign countries for tens of years. However, no private enterprise in China had adopted such technology then. Most of them were still relying on the traditional BF process, a highly energy-consuming technology.

In order to import the RKEF technology, Tsingshan invited the well-known China ENFI Engineering Co., Ltd. to do the engineering planning, and went overseas to learn from foreign steel manufacturers. In 2009, a RKEF-based ferronickel production line invested by Tsingshan was commenced in Wanwu Peninsula, Fu An. As the first RKEF ferronickel production line with independent intellectual property rights in China, it was completed and put into operation in just 18 months, and was quickly reproduced and promoted in China. The production line could not only improve production efficiency, but also achieve clean and environmental protection goals and realized energy conservation and emission reduction.

As driven by the concepts of innovation and green development, Tsingshan created the "RKEF+AOD" (Rotary Kiln Electric Furnace + Argon Oxygen Decarburization) process. This was a cross-discipline technological innovation by which the smelted nickel produced in the RKEF process was not cooled, but was directly sent to the AOD furnace. In this way, the heat consumption and production cost were reduced significantly. Compared with the traditional production process, the RKEF+AOD process helped Tsingshan save 7.2 billion kW·h of electricity per year, which was equivalent to the total electricity consumption of 4 million population cities in one year. Besides, it contributed to an annual reduction of 2 million tons of carbon dust, 7.2 million tons of carbon dioxide, 220,000 tons of sulfur dioxide and 110,000 tons of nitrogen oxides.

Tsingshan takes innovation as the drive for its fast development and sustainable development as its relentless pursuit. After the "RKEF+AOD" process was created, Tsingshan embarked on the application innovation of the "duplex" technology that integrates nickel sulfide ore smelting and the RKEF process. In 2014, an RMB 20 million sulphuric acid plant invested by Tsingshan was completed and put into trial operation, and the nickel sulfide, after treatment, was innovatively applied to the RKEF process. Relying on this technical innovation, productivity was improved, energy consumption was significantly reduced, and harmless treatment of emissions was realized. The flue gas generated in the production process was fully recycled and diluted to obtain sulfuric acid, which may be used in subsequent production. The dust emitted may also be fully recycled to be used in the RKEF process for preparation of crude nickel alloy, which greatly reduced the waste of resources. In addition, nickel sulfide ore released substantial heat energy in the process of roasting, Tsingshan converted it into mechanical energy or electric energy, which greatly reduced the energy consumption and realized self-supply of the most energy. It represented another significant progress in the way of green and sustainable development of Tsingshan. All of these technological innovations, investments, and management improvements demonstrated the environmental protection commitments of Tsingshan.

## 2. Energy Conservation and Emission Reduction: Waste Heat Power Generation and Transportation by Belt Conveyor

Tsingshan is making constant efforts to speed up its transition from a resource-consuming enterprise to a resource-conserving and environment-friendly enterprise. Reducing energy consumption and minimizing waste emission have always been Tsingshan's efforts.

In 2011, Tsingshan first came into contact with the large-scale industrial waste heat and pressure recovery technology from an energy enterprise in Shanghai. Through deep study, Tsingshan found that the waste heat power generation technology could make use of waste to generate value. If used reasonably, it would be the most effective way of waste heat recycling.

After over one year's transformation and construction, Tsingshan installed the waste heat power generation equipment with an installed capacity of 15MW in 2013. The waste heat boiler could absorb and heat the waste heat of flue gas generated in the production process, and convert it into steam to produce mechanical energy which was converted by the generator to electricity. The annual power generation of the waste heat power generation equipment reached 100 million kW·h.

Thereafter, Tsingshan expanded the scope of the application of waste heat power generation projects. It built four similar projects in 2016. And in 2018, the hoods of AOD furnaces of Tsingshan were all upgraded from water-cooling technology to vaporization cooling technology, which further improved the efficiency of energy conversion and recycling.

In addition to the waste heat power generation projects, Tsingshan also created a new mode of building workshops in mining area. In Indonesia, Tsingshan built workshops in the mining area, which turned the desolate mining area into a clean, beautiful and busy industrial park. It eliminated the need for long-distance transportation, which saved 10,000 tons of standard coal every year.

Moreover, Tsingshan made constant efforts to maximize the energy recycling and conversion. It made huge investment in the construction of laterite nickel ore belt conveyors, desulfurization towers, and wastewater treatment facilities to maximize energy conservation and emission reduction in production and operation. For example, Tsingshan invested RMB 200 million to build laterite nickel ore belt conveyors in Fujian and Guangdong. With the 7.5km long belt conveyor, the laterite nickel ore was transported from the wharf to the factory and then to the workshop. The transportation by belt conveyor formed a closed transportation mode which eliminated the escaping and leakage problems in truck transportation, avoided dust pollution, and protected the environment around the mining area and surrounding areas. Tsingshan also established and improved the online monitoring system for energy consumption and waste emission and demanded more stringent requirements on itself. For example, the sulfur content in flue gas of Tsingshan was far lower than the national emission standards.

## 3. Recycling of Resources: Plastic Particles Project and Recycling of Waste Stainless Steel

Tsingshan has always adhered to the economic cycle concept in production process, and has maximized the recycling of waste gas, waste water and solid waste in the production process.

In the production process based on the duplex "RKEF+ nickel sulphide ore", the acid plant needs to purchase packaging bags to package the nickel concentrate. But the disposal of waste packaging bags is rather troublesome because the waste plastic bags usually carry much nickel concentrate which will cause heavy metal pollution if they are washed directly. It is contrary to the commitment to the environmental protection of Tsingshan.

To solve this problem, Tsingshan investigated multiple methods and finally it selected to compress the waste packaging bags into plastic particles. Tsingshan formally commenced its plastic particles project in the acid plant. It built 900 m$^2$ workshop and the project was put into operation in October of that year. Although Tsingshan encountered many difficulties in the commissioning of the plastic particle project, including the production process, siting and other issues, it overcame these difficulties by keeping the corporate social responsibility in environmental protection in mind. Following the plastic particles project, Tsingshan also introduced the water circulation system to avoid sewage discharge. It never stopped its efforts in environmental protection.

The plastic particle project of the acid plant generated considerable market benefits, and realized recycling of resources, the most important goal. The water used for washing the waste package contained 2500—3500mg/L nickel ore. The water is poured into the ferronickel for evaporation and smelting, and then finally applied in the production of stainless steel. Waste packaging causes serious environmental pollution problems if not treated properly. With the plastic particle technology, both nickel ore and water resources are fully recycled and ultimately realized zero emission and ecological environment protection.

As one of the leading stainless steel manufacturers in the world, Tsingshan has always placed green management and sustainable development at the core of its development over the 30 years since its founding. Over the decades, Tsingshan has demonstrated its green development concept to the world by making innovations in smelting technology, practicing energy conservation and reduction of energy consumption and emission, and carrying out recycling of resources. Instead of blind pursuit of economic profits, Tsingshan actively undertakes its social responsibilities to ensure compliance with environmental protection requirements. For Tsingshan, economic interest and environmental responsibilities are both important.

## *Questions*

1. Based on the case, explain the concept of green management and how Tsingshan conducts green management.

2. Which activities did Tsingshan carry out to practice the sustainable development concept? How did Tsingshan benefit from these activities?

## *Tips for Answering the Questions*

1. From the perspectives of green management of enterprise, green actions, corporate culture, mission, vision, and core values, analyze the green management activities carried out by Tsingshan and the significance of green management.

【Should Organizations Be Socially Involved】

2. From the perspective of sustainable development of enterprise, analyze the environmental protection behaviors conducted by Tsingshan in all aspects. Describe which sustainable development activities were carried out by Tsingshan, and the influences of these activities on the economic and non-economic benefits of Tsingshan.

# Case 5

## "Orange Initiative" of Teckon Foundation

## Case Description

In August 2011, Gong Haoqiang, the founder of Teckon Hotel, a local enterprise in Ningbo, led the Hotel to set up the Teckon Foundation. Since then, the Teckon Foundation "Orange Initiative" volunteer activities were officially launched, and Teckon Hotel has taken the initiative to care for left-behind children and bring them warmth. "Orange Initiative" is based on Bing Xin's essay "Little Orange Lamp", which aims to illuminate hope with a touch of warm orange, to open the gate to the outside world and light up a different grow-up path for children. The assistance targets of the "Orange Initiative" are called Orange Star, and the volunteers are called Oranges. As of 2021, the "Orange Initiative" has brought together more than 200 volunteers, serving a total of 3,525 left-behind children, with service time of more than 40,000 hours. The covered regions include Jilin, Yunnan, Guizhou, Heilongjiang, Guangxi, and Hunan province, etc. The "Orange Initiative" has been continuous for more than ten years and has become improved noticeably over time.

### 1. Three Core Programs for Comprehensive Support

In July 2013, Teckon Foundation focused on the left-behind children in the families of service industry employees, and formed the "Orange Initiative" charity activity system, which centers on the three major programs of "study assistance, grow-up guidance, and happy experience camp." The programs target children, mainly from Grade 1 of primary school to Grade 3 of high school. Children who have become Orange Star would receive direct benefit from programs of "study assistance, grow-up guidance, and happy experience camp" which enable them to grow up happily.

Study assistance: Material assistance is provided to each Orange Star every year. Not only does it help the children to go through the difficulties of schooling in the form of bursaries, but it also provides wish cards for children to help them realize their wishes.

Grow-up guidance: Help the Orange Star communicate with their parents. Through the one-on-one "pair up" between Orange and Orange Star, it provide the children with emotional guidance and communication and help them to establish a good and healthy psychological environment. At the same time, through the parental consultation hotline for left-behind children, they guide parents how to communicate with children, so as to build the bridge of communication between children and parents. In addition, the "Orange Initiative" leverages the parents schools established by the government, enterprises, professional organizations and other social welfare forces to open up two-way grow-up guidance between children and parents. At the same time, online and offline classes for parents' schools are available to break the time and space limitations of traditional classrooms and expand the audience group through remote interaction.

Happy experience camp: A summer camp for the Orange Star is held every summer vacation. Every year, 30 to 50 left-behind children are invited to Ningbo to reunite with their parents and participate in a 7-day summer camp. Different course experience contents are designed according to the annual themes and the characteristics of children's age groups, including traditional culture, feeling Ningbo, psychological and physical health education, safety education, role-play, military training, natural Ningbo, humanities of Ningbo, Yangming Traditional Culture Academy, patriotism education, which allow children to experience Ningbo in all-round through "visual, auditory, tactile, sensory and gustatory" ways. At the same time, through the occupational experience of "working with parents", they can feel the hard work of their parents, which strengthens the emotional communication and mutual understanding with parents and opens up a window to the outside world for the children. The purpose of the summer camp is to provide a "happy experience". It strives to bring an unforgettable and joyful journey for the children, whether it is "wish time" to fulfill children's wishes or team-building interactive games.

In addition to the three core programs, Teckon Foundation also actively participates in public welfare advocacy activities, calling on the public to care for the left-behind children. Teckon Foundation has also earmarked funds for research and book publishing on left-behind children, and has funded the publication of *Be With You: Report on Left-behind Children in China* and other publications. Teckon Foundation regularly organizes good causes forums, charity dinners and other activities to attract more attention from society, encourage more people to discuss and participate in the cause of caring for left-behind children. They also prepare and shoot documentaries for left-behind children to draw attention to the mental health, safety and education of youth and children.

## 2. The Volunteer Team Continues to Grow

In August 2014, in order to better serve charitable activities, Orange Club was established under "Orange Initiative" to set up Orange selection and professional training system as well as a comprehensive volunteer recruitment, training and management plan. They gradually expanded the volunteer team from Ningbo to the various locations of left-behind children, breaking the limitation of long-distance communication.

Since the "Orange Initiative" was launched, the Orange team has also been expanding. At present, the volunteers of "Orange Initiative" include not only volunteers from Teckon Foundation, but also college student volunteers and social volunteers who are passionate about volunteer activities, willing to help and care for others. The Oranges of the "Orange Initiative" include: Short term volunteers—provide short-term service support during program activities; Pair volunteers—provide long-term one-on-one grow-up guidance and assistance for children; Resource volunteers—provide resources support, such as media resources, teaching and research resources; Star volunteers—experts or key opinion leaders in various fields to promote the programs.

Outside Ningbo, the first local volunteer team was established under the "Orang Initiative" in southwestern Guizhou in April 2018 and the second was established in Yanbian Korean Autonomous Prefecture in August 2020. Thereafter more local volunteer teams were set up to implement the "Orange Initiative" program in more regions.

### 3. "Orange Initiative" Entered Liangshan, Sichuan

In 2021, Ningbo pair up with Liangshan, Sichuan for the assistance of children in poor families. As a member of China Charities Aid Foundation for Children, Teckon Foundation actively responded to the call and invited excellent children in Liangshan who were from poor families, to join the pair-up program and became Orange Stars in the "Orange Initiative".

The volunteer team visited the families of some students, expressed concern and condolences, and offered scholarships of thousands of yuan and sent invitation letters to the happy experience camp. Relying on the comprehensive good causes ecological chain model of the "Orange Initiative", the pair-up assistance program helped the Orange Stars in Jinyang, Liangshan to improve the living environment, family environment and social public opinion environment in an all-rounded way and help the children to build healthy personalities of self-confidence, self-reliance and self-improvement.

Gradually, with endeavors of the local volunteer team, the material resources and spiritual care of Ningbo were transmitted to every Orange Star family in Jinyang, successfully bringing the Ningbo Model of caring for left-behind children to Liangshan.

From 2011 to 2022, it has been eleven years since Teckon Foundation launched the "Orange Initiative". Based on years of accumulated experience in "Orange Initiative" charitable activities, Teckon Foundation created a comprehensive good causes ecological chain of caring for left-behind children. The ecological chain covers left-behind children, their parents, volunteers, the public and other relevant groups, and provides a model for the social issue of "how to help left-behind children". It has been evaluated by the government as the Ningbo Model and Ningbo Method for caring for left-behind children. In September 2016, the "Orange Initiative" of Teckon Foundation stood out among 302 outstanding annual brand marketing cases across the country and won the 15th "China Outstanding Brand Marketing Award". Teckon Foundation has contributed its own strength to solving the social problem of left-behind children.

## Questions

1. Is Teckon Foundation "Orange Initiative" a result of social obligation, social response, or social responsibility?

2. From management's perspective, what benefits has the "Orange Initiative" brought to Teckon Hotel?

## Tips for Answering the Questions

1. This case focuses on the charity work of Teckon Foundation. It describes the initiation, development, achievements and significance of the charity, showing the history, changes and effects of Teckon Foundation "Orange Initiative". The key knowledge points involved: the concepts of social obligation, social responsiveness and social responsibility, as well as the factors that affect decision-making on corporate social responsibility.

【Social Obligation? Social Responsiveness? Social Responsibility?】

2. From the manager's perspective, analyze the organizational moral behavior involved in "Orange Initiative", summarize several periods of organizational morality of Teckon Hotel and the characteristics of each period, and analyze the benefits that organizational morality and corporate social responsibility have brought to Teckon Hotel in connection with its strategy, mission, vision and organizational culture.

# Case 6

## Inheritance and Innovation of Gang Ya Gou

## *Case Description*

Gang Ya Gou is a food brand mainly selling sweet dumplings (or Tangyuans). There is an old saying that has spread among Ningbo people for years, "wake up at the midnight, go to Gang Ya Gou for sweet dumplings. Still unwilling to leave after eating a bowl, and ask for another and another bowl of sweet dumplings," reflecting how local people are fond of Gang Ya Gou sweet dumplings.

In 1926, Jiang Dingfa from Ningbo set up a stall in Chenghuang Temple to sell sweet dumplings. Soon after, he opened a shop in Kaiming Street and named the shop Gang Ya Gou, pronounced the same as his nickname Jiang A Gou in Ningbo dialect. Thus, a brand logo with a vat, a duck and a yellow dog was created. In 1993, Gang Ya Gou was awarded China Time-honored Brand by the Ministry of Commerce. In 1997, Gang Ya Gou sweet dumplings were recognized as Chinese famous snacks by China Cuisine Association.

After the reform and opening up, as foreign brands of fast food came to China, the glory of the traditional brand Gang Ya Gou gradually faded. In 2007, Gang Ya Gou had to close the 10-year prosperous shop in the food street of Chenghuang Temple due to the reconstruction of the old city, its business area dwindled to just 100 m$^2$ from 1,200 m$^2$ overnight, and the brand was faced with being taken over by other brands. Chen Kaihe, a native of Ningbo, with his passion for this traditional brand and his ambition of reviving the brand, managed to coordinate all parties and then persuaded the shareholders of Gang Ya Gou into selling 100% equities of the brand to him. In 2009, Chen kaihe became the new boss of Gang Ya Gou.

## 1. Revival of Gang Ya Gou Brand

After taking over Gang Ya Gou, Chen Kaihe faced many problems, among which the increase in operating cost, the decline in quality, and the thinning of profits were particularly prominent. It was urgent to transform customers' stereotyped image of Gang Ya Gou as "a declining old brand" and to achieve brand revival. So he decided to reform the brand: First, carry forward the excellent tradition of the brand and attach importance to the quality of sweet dumplings; Second, reconstruct the supply chain system and broaden marketing channels; Third, investigate the market demand, and adjust the marketing strategy and product categories accordingly.

Chen Kaihe believes that in addition to the long history and the meaning of reunion, the reason why Gang Ya Gou has been popular among Ningbo people is that Gang Ya Gou has strictly followed the six traditional processes of material selection, soaking, grinding, pressing, stuffing and cooking. Sweet dumplings with black sesame lard fillings have always been the most famous among all products of Gang Ya Gou, which are made with black sesame seeds that are oily, sweet but not greasy. Back then, Jiang Dingfa, the founder of Gang Ya Gou, was extremely fastidious in selecting raw materials of sweet dumplings, including the local first-class white glutinous rice flour and high-quality thick leaf lard of pigs. In addition, Gang Ya Gou has traditionally adopted the water milling process, in which the glutinous rice is changed from solid to liquid and then resolidified by pressing and steaming. The water milling process not only makes the best flavor of the glutinous rice, but also ensures the tender and smooth taste of sweet dumplings skins. The process of making sweet dumplings by hand, however, is very complicated. If even glutinous rice is freshly ground, the cost will rise largely as a sewage treatment system alone will cost millions of RMB. Chen Kaihe thought over and finally decided to keep the water milling process. He thought that the water milling process is the key to maintaining the uniqueness of Gang Ya Gou.

To improve the quality of sweet dumplings, innovation is a must. Chen Kaihe built a high-standard food factory in Jiulong Lake, Zhenhai, set up the Institute of Research on Healthy Food and Biotechnology, purchased many modern machinery, and set uniform standards on food processing.

Improving quality is important for brand revival. Nowadays, it is no longer the era where good wine needs no bush. It is also important to establish efficient and reasonable marketing channels. Chen Kaihe has been thinking about how to make this Ningbo-based sweet dumplings brand successfully go out of Zhejiang and to the dining table of all families all over the country. Relying on only offline shops is far from enough, quick-frozen sweet dumplings shall be launched so that they can be sold in supermarkets.

Through market research, Chen Kaihe found that in China, the quick-frozen food in the market is mainly dumplings and sweet dumplings. In the quick-frozen food sector in 2020, Sanquan, Synear, Longfeng and Wan Chai Pier take up 70% of market shares, among, 27% shares of Sanquan, 20% shares of Synear, 12% shares of Longfeng, and 11% shares of Wan Chai Pier, respectively. In the early days, Gang Ya Gou had also developed quick-frozen sweet dumplings, but because the products were not diverse enough and they were much less competitive than the diversified and serialized quick-frozen food brands such as Sanquan, Synear, Longfeng, and especially with the rapid rising of local brands such as Sanxue, Gang Ya Gou and the memory it left were gradually weakened, and thus Gang Ya Gou was soon expelled out of the quick-frozen sweet dumplings market. Nowadays, the competition in the quick-frozen sweet dumplings industry is becoming increasingly fierce, and it is of great importance for Gang Ya Gou to establish a suitable business model to expand its market.

The popular brands in the market such as Sanquan and Synear have low prices. It is obviously infeasible for Gang Ya Gou to compete with them on price or output. Chen Kaihe thought that after the reform and opening up, the level of national consumption has been unprecedentedly improved, and high-quality products are more attractive to customers. Gang Ya Gou is positioned as the highest-end sweet dumplings in Chinese market, and its price must match the quality. "As long as they are worth while, we don't need to worry about marketing." Chen Kaihe said. Therefore, in terms of consumer identification, Gang Ya Gou is targeted at the middle and higher classes. Unlike the quick-frozen sweet dumplings on the market, Gang Ya Gou focuses on middle-end and high-end products, and its average price is twice that of similar products. In the spring of 2015, Gang Ya Gou was introduced into the Century Market, and all its sweet dumplings were sold out even before the arrival of the Lantern Festival. The high quality and high-end brand, the uniqueness and time-honored culture are the foundations to support a higher price of Gang Ya Gou compared with other sweet dumpling brands.

After determining the market position, the next challenge that Chen Kaihe faced was how to sell the quick-frozen sweet dumplings to other cities. Quick-frozen sweet dumplings are prone to collapse and there were other problems which affect quality and appearance Therefore, Gang Ya Gou needs to rebuild a special supply chain to ensure the quality of sweet dumplings. Chen Kaihe found that most of the quick-frozen sweet dumpling manufacturers have signed agreements with some logistics companies, and these cold-chain carriers transported the quick-frozen sweet dumplings from the factory to various shopping malls, during which, however, the sweet dumplings are inevitable to crack due to shock. Instead, Haagen-Dazs, an internationally renowned ice cream brand, adopts constant-temperature cold-chain transportation from the factory to end of the sales, and distributes its products centrally from the central kitchen to various restaurants, which is safer and more efficient. Therefore Chen Kaihe finally decided to establish Gang Ya Gou's cold-chain transportation system in the same way Haagen-Dazs has done.

In addition to introducing quick-frozen sweet dumplings into large supermarkets, Chen Kaihe has also adjusted the marketing channels. Based on sales in supermarkets, Gang Ya Gou also opens its own shops and cooperates with many well-known catering brands such as Haidilao, Lixiangguo, HEYTEA, etc., and also provides direct delivery service for high-end hotels such as Hilton, New Century, and Cordis.

## 2. Digital Transformation of Gang Ya Gou

With the booming of E-commerce in China, many enterprises have entered the digital era. Online platforms such as Taobao, JD.com, and Hema are very popular among consumers for their convenient and fast shopping experiences, leading to a significant decline in sales of traditional offline supermarkets. The food industry, where Gang Ya Gou is located is also facing the impact of digital transformation.

Chen Kaihe decided to carry out digital transformation, and formulated a four-step development strategy: First, achieve digital access through online platforms, and increase the sales and collect data with the aid of large sales platforms; Second, implement digital marketing, for example, raise the brand awareness and attract consumers on Xiaohongshu App and other channels; Third, carry out digital R&D of popular food categories in the market based on big data; Fourth, build a digital operation platform that integrates the production, sales, finance and management of Gang Ya Gou to facilitate the digitalization of operation and management.

In 2016, Gang Ya Gou started to sell its sweet dumplings on Taobao and other E-commerce platforms to expand online sales channels. In the same year, it cooperated with Hema in the hope of entering the national market. Different from a traditional supermarket, Hema, an emerging retail platform, adopts a digital management mode. It can feed back more operational and forecast data to enterprises and provide data support for their product innovation. Based on Hema's big data and consumer survey, Chen Kaihe found that the 16 sweet dumplings packed per bag were difficult for most consumers to finish in one meal and were prone to waste. Consumers favored samll-sized, feature-rich, and convenient foods. Therefore, he decided to provide small-package sweet dumplings for Hema. In 2018, the sales of Gang Ya Gou on Hema surged by about 15 times.

Data is an important tool for Chen Kaihe to make effective decisions. Gang Ya Gou has not only sought to attract consumers with the aid of Tik Tok, Xiaohongshu, Weibo and other platforms but also constantly analyzed customers' demands and preferences. In view that the target consumers are young people, Gang Ya Gou designed new flavors of quick-frozen sweet dumplings, including durian, matcha, sorghum-milk-egg, and rose, as well as special foods such as handmade wine, sugar-made osmanthus and instant steamed stuffed buns. Chen Kaihe noticed that young people who are usually busy with their studies and work are the consumer groups that the old brands are hard to reach. Because they are more willing to place orders on a take-out App. To reach them, Gang Ya Gou needs to provide take-out service on online platforms. In 2020, the Gang Ya Gou take-out applet was put into trial operation, and received nearly 10,000 orders (worth RMB 493,000) in the first month, which were not only from old customers, but also from new customers who first knew Gang Ya Gou.

In 2021, Gang Ya Gou cooperated with Weimob to build an integrated marketing mode that combines WeChat take-out applet, online shops, and offline shops. Chen Kaihe wished to take advantage of the integrated membership ecology to familiarize the young consumers with the Gang Ya Gou brand and then divert resources from the public domain platforms to the private domain applet. There have been about 300,000 members who have registered on the WeChat take-out applet in 2021. Since online digital sales were deployed, the sales of Gang Ya Gou have seen a continuous rise.

In addition, Chen Kaihe has also attached great importance to the digital transformation of business management. Due to the many data transmission barriers that existed when the management team of Gang Ya Gou used Enterprise WeChat for daily office communication, it increased the management cost. Therefore, Gang Ya Gou is committed to building a digital base of the enterprise and integrating the production data, sales data, financial data, partner data and store sales data in one system to greatly improve management efficiency and assist managers in making scientific decisions.

The digital transformation of business management will be an important part of the transformation of Gang Ya Gou in the upcoming years, and it is undoubtedly the key to the continuous innovation and vitality of the brand.

## Questions

1. What key decisions were made and how were they made in this case?

2. Analyze how the managers of Gang Ya Gou made decisions based on big data.

## *Tips for Answering the Questions*

1. In this case, a series of key decisions were made, including inheritance of the watermill process, R&D of quick-frozen products, sales at online platforms, take-out service, development of augmented products, etc., which keeps the old brand Gang Ya Gou improving continuously. During analysis, combine the relevant knowledge of different types of decisions and different thinking modes of managers. For example, decision-making can be divided into routine decision-making and non-routine decision-making. Managers have two different modes of thinking: linear thinking and nonlinear thinking. Linear thinking prefers to process information using external data and through rational and logical thinking. Nonlinear thinking prefers to process information using internal information and with insight, feelings and intuition.

【Decision Making: Rationality? Intuition? Bounded Rationality?】

2. Analyze how product innovation is made based on online data in the case to explain the role of big data in the decision-making process and correctly understand the relationship between big data and decision-making. Big data is a powerful tool to assist managers in decision-making. However, no matter how comprehensive the big data is or how deep the analysis is, good judgment from managers is still needed for coordination.

# Case 7

## New Product Development at Ningbo Cixing

## Case Description

Ningbo Cixing Co., Ltd. (hereinafter referred to as Cixing), founded in 1988, is a listed enterprise in China's computerized flat knitting machine industry. It is the implementation unit of the National Torch Program and has won the second prize of the National Science and Technology Progress Award. In 2021, the KS series fully formed computerized flat knitting machine developed by Cixing overturned the knitting process of the traditional flat knitting machine, realized the one-time forming of knitted sweaters, represented the current cutting-edge computerized flat knitting machine technology. Cixing planned to enter the field of fully formed computerized flat knitting machine in 2010, and finally developed the KS series fully formed computerized flat knitting machine, which represents the highest level in the industry, in 2021. Over the past 10 years, Cixing has held on to its goal without letting go, carefully planned and deployed, and finally achieved a major technical breakthrough and market success.

## 1. Enter the Field of Fully Formed Computerized Flat Knitting Machine through M&A

With the rise of 3D printing, artificial intelligence and other technologies, as well as the impact of factors such as rising labor costs and the shortage of workers in the sewing process, some leading enterprises in the industry began to research the fully formed computerized flat knitting machine.[1]

For example, in 1999, Shima Seiki first developed the four needle plates fully formed computerized flat knitting machine and applied for a patent. In 2003, Stoll launched the two

---

[1] From the perspective of the technological evolution of the industry worldwide, the flat knitting machine has gone through three generations of different technological paradigms: hand flat knitting machine (1900—1960), computerized flat knitting machine (1960—2000) and fully formed computerized flat knitting machine (2000 to the present).

needle plates fully formed computerized flat knitting machine. Full formed technology can not only reduce the sewing process to save labor costs, but also greatly reduce waste yarn in production and improve the comfort of clothing. Therefore, it has gradually become a new technical development direction in the flat knitting machine industry. However, due to the high cost of the fully formed computerized flat knitting machines, which mainly target high-end customers, the market demand is small. Therefore, the mainstream models in the global market before 2018 were still computerized flat knitting machines. As the leading enterprise in the domestic flat knitting machine industry, Cixing began to pay attention to full formed technology in 2010. At that time, there were many full formed technology designs on the market, such as two needle plates, four needle plates and five needle plates.

In 2008, the global financial crisis broke out, and Steiger, the world's third largest manufacturer of computerized flat knitting machines, was struggling to find buyers, which brought Cixing a rare opportunity to rapidly improve its full formed technology through M&A. In 2010, Cixing successfully acquired Steiger, and received its R&D team and advanced technology.

At the early stage of the merger, Cixing did not have the independent research and development capability of the fully formed computerized flat knitting machine, and the computerized flat knitting machine was still the largest main business of the company at that time. Therefore, after discussion, the company's senior executives unanimously decided to let Steiger independently take charge of the research and development of the fully formed computerized flat knitting machine, and make improvements based on its existing technology. Cixing was only responsible for the subsequent debugging and assembly.

For Cixing at the early stage of the acquisition, the development of fully formed computerized flat knitting machines by Steiger was a strategic plan with the lowest cost and highest return. The fact also proved that the plan had achieved good results. In 2012, Cixing obtained an invention patent on full formed technology, produced an engineering prototype in 2015, and trial-produced the first full formed computerized flat knitting machine Taurus in 2017. As soon as Cixing's Taurus was exhibited, it was called a milestone design in the knitwear industry, and hailed as opening a new direction for the domestic knitting industry.

However, Cixing encountered difficulties in promoting the fully formed computerized flat knitting machine in the market. Although Cixing has domestic high-quality marketing channels and sales networks, and has accumulated a large amount of marketing knowledge, because Taurus uses a composite needle design, the cost is very high. A needle costs 100 yuan, 10 times the price of ordinary needles, and it is inconvenient to change needles, so it can not meet the price positioning and operation needs of domestic customers for the fully formed computerized flat knitting machine. Therefore, in the market, compared with the fully formed computerized flat knitting machine of Shima Seiki and other companies, it is not competitive. Although Cixing's first attempt in the fully formed computerized flat knitting machine market ended in failure, it has also accumulated a lot of experience in the research and development of fully formed computerized flat knitting machines.

## 2. Achieve Product Innovation Success Through Joint Research and Development

In 2017, due to the rise in labor costs and the need for enterprise transformation and upgrading, downstream knitting enterprises' demand for fully formed computerized flat knitting machines with a higher degree of automation increased significantly, but many enterprises were reluctant to invest in research and development due to the high price of fully formed computerized flat knitting machines. Cixing is keenly aware of this market demand, and decides to vigorously promote the research and development of fully formed computerized flat knitting machines and reduce the manufacturing cost as much as possible.

At the beginning of 2018, Cixing decided to jointly research and develop the fully formed computerized flat knitting machine by the domestic R&D Department and Steiger, and adopted two plans for parallel research and design: on the one hand, the domestic R&D Department and Steiger continued to promote the design of the four needle plates composite needle; On the other hand, the domestic Technology Research and Development Department independently developed a new structure of two needle plates plus ordinary needles. In the same year, Cixing established a full molding research institute, which is mainly responsible for structural design, process research and the development of plate making system.

In order to accelerate the R&D process, Cixing strengthened its collaboration with Steiger. The domestic and foreign R&D teams communicate frequently. The foreign teams need to report the progress to the domestic technical director regularly. At the same time, the domestic teams actively invite Swiss experts to China for trial production and debugging of the machine. Within the company, all departments work together to gather all forces and form a closed loop. For example, after the new model is developed, the Technology Department conducts proofing for the new machine, tests its function and stability, and feeds back the problems found in the test and improvement suggestions to the R&D Department. After the R&D Department makes functional improvements, the Technology Department confirms them, and improves the machine's performance through continuous feedback and interaction.

After nearly a year's efforts, the two needle plates full formed computerized flat knitting machine KS3-72 was the first to be successfully developed. This kind of machine used a special pulling component "needle rake", and the composite needle was successfully replaced by a common needle, which greatly reduced the cost. In addition, after the commercialization of Taurus failed, Cixing found that the original plate making system of Steiger was not suitable for the habits of Chinese masters, so it cooperated with Steiger to redevelop the Model plate-making software, which changed the style of the software and made it more suitable for the operating habits of Chinese masters. In order to achieve mass production of the fully formed computerized flat knitting machines, Cixing invested in the construction of an intelligent manufacturing workshop of fully formed computerized flat knitting machines in 2019. After mass production, Cixing two needle plates full formed computerized flat knitting machine quickly occupied most of the domestic market with a price only one-third that of similar products from Shima Seiki. However, at this time, Cixing still has a certain gap to close in the field of high-end fully formed computerized flat knitting machine with Shima Seiki.

## 3. Create New Technological Advantages Through Design Supplement Strategy

In order to cope with the competition from Cixing, Shima Seiki also launched its own two needle plates full formed computerized flat knitting machine, engaging in direct design competition with Cixing. To consolidate the fully formed technology with independent intellectual property rights, Cixing gradually adjusted its previous technical strategy and adopted the technical strategy of design supplement, which involved continuously optimizing and improving its core technology.

The technology strategy of design supplement requires the company to continuously launch new products, thus forming a leading paradigm of technology and shaping technological advantages that other companies cannot imitate. In order to seize the market opportunity, Cixing has formulated rich incentive measures to reward and commend the departments and employees who exceeded the targets.

With clear goals and thorough plans, Cixing has finally realized the serialization of fully formed computerized flat knitting machines. In terms of architecture design, on the one hand, Cixing has successively developed 13.2, 4.2, 6.2 inch and other models of different specifications based on the original 10.2 inch two needle plates model; On the other hand, based on Steiger four needle plates technology, Cixing changed the original composite needle into a common needle, and improved the traction device. In 2019, Cixing developed a new fully formed five needle bed design, which greatly reduced the equipment cost while achieving the effect of eighteen needle knitting. In terms of component development, Cixing mainly replaced expensive composite needles with ordinary needles, and pioneered the eighteen needle technology in China, which can realize full stitch weaving and maximize high-density weaving. In addition, Cixing further optimized the independent control system of the electric yarn mouth on the KS3 product, enabling it to move freely in the horizontal direction, so that the yarn mouth can be accurately positioned and fed synchronously. Through the optimization and upgrading of components, the quality of Cixing fully formed computerized flat knitting machine has been further improved, the cost has been further reduced, and the products are more competitive in the market.

In 2019 and 2020, Cixing sold more than 2600 fully formed computerized flat knitting machines, with a market share of 20%. It is expected that its market share will reach 35% by 2025, and it is expected to become a global leader in the field of fully formed computerized flat knitting machines.

## Question

1. What role does the goal play in changing the strategic direction of Cixing's Plan?

2. In the fully formed computerized flat knitting machine industry, what types of plans need to be formulated when enterprises develop new products?

3. In this case, what factors will affect the plan of senior managers?

4. In the process of developing into a leading enterprise in the industry, what challenges might Cixing's executives face? How should they respond?

## Tips for Answering the Questions

1. Goals can provide direction and guidance for management decisions and actions, and constitute a standard for measuring actual effects. Goal-oriented management is one of the most widely used management methods. A large number of examples have proved that clear goals can play an incentive role in changing the direction of enterprise planning strategies. It can improve the management level, help managers to distinguish organizational tasks and structures, and authorize

【Establishing Goals】

according to the expected results of people's tasks. It can encourage employees to strive to achieve their own goals and organizational goals. It is helpful to establish an effective control mechanism, measure the results and take corrective actions. The above target management knowledge can be combined with the development process of Cixing full formed computerized flat knitting machine for analysis.

2. According to the width, time frame, specificity and frequency of use of the plan, the plan can be divided into strategic plan and operational plan, short-term plan and long-term plan, guiding plan and specific plan, as well as one-time plan and continuous plan. It can be analyzed in combination with the above scheme classification method and the characteristics of the fully formed computerized flat knitting machine industry.

3. The process of formulating plans will be affected by three contingency factors, namely, the organizational level, the degree of uncertainty of the environment and the duration of future commitments. At the organizational level, senior managers think more about issues from a macro perspective, mainly making strategic plans. In terms of the degree of environmental uncertainty, when the degree of uncertainty is high, managers must be ready to respond to changes or make changes to the plan during the implementation process. In terms of the duration of future commitments, the plan should be extended to a sufficiently long term in the future.

4. In the process of becoming a leading enterprise in the industry, the external environment is constantly changing, and enterprise executives may encounter situations where the original plan no longer works. Enterprise executives should formulate specific but flexible plans in an uncertain environment. Even in the face of a very uncertain environment, they still need to formulate formal plans to assess organizational performance, and establish a more flat organizational level to help enterprises make more effective decisions in a dynamic environment.

# Case 8

## The Transformation and Upgrading Process of Hailun Piano

## *Case Description*

Founded in 2001, Hailun Piano Co., Ltd. (hereinafter referred to as Hailun Piano) is primarily engaged in the manufacturing of pianos. It is a key high-tech enterprise of the national Torch Plan and a key cultural export enterprise of China. As a well-known brand in China, the upright and grand pianos made by Hailun Piano have been widely recognized and praised around the world, with a significant presence in Europe, the United States, Japan, etc. Hailun Piano also provides education and training based on smart pianos as their newly developing business. In 2019, Hailun Piano cooperated with the College Continuing Education of Central Conservatory of Music (CCOM) and launched the College Continuing Education of CCOM & Hailun Smart Piano Experimental Classroom program. The program is intended to provide training and instructions for teachers of Hailun Pianos' franchisees relying on teaching materials developed by the powerful faculty of CCOM, to help combine teaching and grade examinations and improve the piano teaching outcomes. The program marked the beginning of a new era of art education and piano teaching. As a private enterprise, Hailun Piano started from scratch and has completed the transition from a manufacturer of parts and pianos to a service provider.

## 1. First Generation Starts up: From the Parts Production to Piano Making

Before founding Hailun Piano, Mr. Chen Hailun operated a metal accessories factory and supplied parts to domestic piano manufacturers, which are mainly located in Guangzhou, Shanghai, Yingkou, and Beijing. Chen had a dream to take his factory to the next level. So he turned his eyes to the "engine" of pianos—the soundboard, a core component of pianos. Such a transition meant an upgrade of the factory's main products, which required an advanced production line with national leading technologies and workmanship. This posed great challenges in talent, technology, and manufacturing equipment. Fortunately, Chen got technology support from the Beijing Hsinghai Piano Group and Wendl & Lung. Besides,

Chen imported the advanced, expensive five-axis linkage machine tool from Japan. Chen completed the upgrade of his factory in 2002, only one year after he bought the equipment in 2001. In March 2003, Chen showcased his soundboard products at the German Frankfurt musical instrument exhibition and received widespread recognition from foreign piano manufacturers. But also at that time, he found that foreign manufacturers took the long view and were willing to invest a lot to ensure consistently superior quality. This made Chen know the importance of technical experts. Since then, Chen has spent a lot of money on engaging experts for technical support, and the remuneration of talents even cost half of the company's annual profit.

The transformation from soundboards to pianos was a milestone in the history of Hailun Piano. To avoid competition with domestic established manufacturers, Chen still supplied piano parts in the Chinese market while selling their pianos to Europe, which also helped test the quality of their pianos. In 2004, the 500 pianos made by Hailun Piano were all accepted by the Europe market. Chen then closed the accessories business, registered the trademark "HAILUN", and established Hailun Piano. In 2005, Hailun Piano formally entered the Chinese market. As of 2019, Hailun Piano's annual sales volume reached 105,000 units, ranking 4th globally, and was one of the top three bestselling brands in the Chinese market. Hailun Piano was listed on the Shenzhen Stock Exchange in 2012. The development philosophy of "slowly but steadily" established by the 1st generation of Hailun Piano profoundly influenced the entrepreneurial goal of the successor, and Hailun Piano began a new journey.

## 2. Two Generations Collaboration: From Piano Making to the Development of Smart Pianos

The R&D of smart pianos had been put on the agenda since the listing of Hailun Piano in 2012, and fully embodied the efforts of the two generations. In 2010, Chen Chaofeng, the only son of Chen Hailun joined the company. His working experience in software development made him the most suitable person to lead the development of smart pianos.

Chen Chaofeng did not immediately start management work but instead rotated through the factory workshops. After understanding the piano making process, he was responsible for IPO and investment of Hailun Piano. During the construction of the new workshop, Chen Chaofeng presided over the process design of the production line. Through learning and hardworking, Chen Chaofeng's abilities significantly improved. In 2013, he began to take charge of the R&D of smart pianos under the direction of the first generation leader.

Hailun Piano was a newcomer to the smart piano field, although it held a leading position in traditional piano manufacturing. As a start-up organization, Chen Chaofeng and his team achieved fruitful achievements. After the failure of cooperation with the Beijing University of Posts and Telecommunications, Chen Chaofeng started to build his own R&D team with great support from his father. On the one hand, Chen chaofeng and his team drew on experience from Europe and the United States, and dug deep into audio synchronization and current noise. Facing challenges such as unstable chip performance during the innovative attempts, Chen Chaofeng and his team optimized their design repeatedly and finally created a proven product. On the other hand, they were improving the remote music communication feature. Due to the unique sound quality requirements of smart pianos, conventional networks would not satisfy the needs of the instruments. With 5G networks, Hailun smart pianos can ensure synchronization in remote music transmission and therefore lossless audio sound, which is a great advantage. In addition, Chen Chaofeng and his team were tasked with developing an automatic performance function, that is, when someone plays a piece of music online, other person can reproduce the performance of the music with consistent strength, key sequence, etc. This function can simplify the teaching process, and is also useful for remote music teaching activities. In 2014, Hailun Piano established a wholly-owned subsidiary Beijing Hailun Network Information Technology Co., Ltd. to provide IT support for the development of smart pianos.

## 3. Second Generation Takes Over: From Smart Pianos to Training Schools

In 2014, Chen Hailun and Chen Chaofeng discussed the future of Hailun Piano, deciding that Chen Hailun would steer the overall direction and Chen Chaofeng would be responsible for the day-to-day operation of Hailun Piano. Then Chen Chaofeng founded the Hailun Art Education and Investment Co., Ltd. to continue the development of smart training aids and explore the art education industry. This marked the transition of Hailun Piano from a piano manufacturer to a service provider. Chen Chaofeng and his father believed there was a big market for art education and training in China, and smart pianos could not only entertain people but also support piano teaching activities. So they established a music training center. The gap in China's art enlightenment education market places smart pianos in a favorable position. Nowadays, the piano is quite popular among children. They spend much time learning to play the piano, which however is usually very boring. As time elapses, children may lose interest. But if they do not spend much time on practice, they would not make progress. In addition, exam-oriented piano education ignores the learning of music basics, which more and more parents are aware of this problem, and attaches more importance to the learning of basic music theory knowledge, instead of blindly pursuing grade certificates. All of these create a favorable environment for education based on smart pianos.

The development of smart pianos towards smart teaching aids lays a good foundation for the art education business of Hailun Piano. Chen Chaofeng and his team have developed an App for one-to-many piano teaching, which can not only reduce the financial burden of parents but also help stimulate children's interest in learning to play the piano through interactive teaching and animations. Hailun Piano created innovative finger-style piano lessons to help children correct mistakes by key indicator lights arranged in different sequences and practice through the App. Also, Hailun Piano has been developing its courses with support from professors of Beijing Normal University, and incorporated these courses into the App for online teaching activities. Besides, Hailun Piano established smart piano classrooms and music training schools. It has set up a pilot music training school through cooperation with Ningbo's colleges and universities, and has inked an agreement with CCOM to jointly develop courses.

The relentless efforts of the two generations pushed Hailun Piano from a small piano parts factory to a giant industry leader. Hailun Piano witnessed the organizational transformation and the family inheritance.

## Questions

1. Analyze the strategic management process according to the part "First Generation Starts up: From the Parts Production to Pianos making".

2. What corporate strategy and competitive strategy did Hailun Piano adopt in its three transformations?

3. Analyze the important role of strategic leadership based on the case content.

## Tips for Answering the Questions

1. The process of strategic management consists of six steps, namely, identifying the organization's current mission, objectives and strategies, conducting external environment analysis, conducting internal analysis, formulating strategies, implementing strategies and evaluating results. In this part, Chen Hailun's strategic management goal is the whole piano manufacturing. Based on the analysis of the internal and external environment, in order to avoid competition with domestic old-brand manufacturers, Hailun Chen adopted the strategy of raising pianos with accessories. All the pianos produced were sold to Europe, and at the same time, the product quality could be better inspected.

2. Corporate strategy is the strategy that determines what businesses a company is engaged in or wants to engage in and how it wants to engage in these businesses, mainly including growth strategy, stability strategy and renewal strategy. Competitive strategy is the strategy that determines how an organization competes in each type of business, including cost leadership strategy,

【Corporate Strategy】

differentiation strategy and focus strategy. In the level of corporate strategy, from the first transformation Hailun Piano adopts vertical integration in the growth strategy, through the forward integration to achieve growth. From the second and the third transformation, Hailun piano adopts the diversification strategy in the growth strategy. In the level of competitive strategy, from the first transformation, Hailun piano took the differentiation strategy, it carried out the quality competition, and chose overseas markets. From the second transformation, Hailun Piano adopts the differentiation strategy and focus strategy, focusing on smart piano products in the piano market and setting up wholly-owned subsidiaries to support technical research and development. From the third transformation, Hailun Piano adopts the differentiation strategy, focusing on the piano teaching function, and developing the product from smart pianos to smart teaching aids.

3. Strategic leadership is the ability to anticipate, envision, remain flexible, think strategically, and work with others in the organization to initiate changes to create a bright future for the organization. There are eight key dimensions for senior managers to provide effective strategic leadership: determining the organization's goals or objectives, developing and maintaining core competitiveness of organizations, developing human capital, creating and maintaining a strong organizational culture, creating and maintaining the organization's various relations, restructuring the mainstream views by questioning various assumptions and asking sharp questions, emphasizing ethical organizational decision-making and decision-making time, and establishing a flexible organizational control system. In this case, both father and son can clearly describe the goals and visions of the organization, and find their strategies through internal and external environment analysis.

# Case 9

## Fenghua's Organizational Restructuring

## *Case Description*

Fenghua Property Services Co. Ltd. (hereinafter referred to as Fenghua) was established in Guangzhou in August 1991 as a private enterprise invested by natural persons. Fenghua engages in property services for offices, government logistics, urban complexes, commercial plazas, residential buildings, and public transportation system services, urban integrated services, public utility services, road cleaning, etc. In recent years, Fenghua has expanded its market territory to 39 cities in 20 provinces. While the company developed rapidly, Mr. Bai, the chairman of Fenghua, was worried that the company didn't have distinctive specialties and lacked professional competence. As its scale increased and businesses varied, the existing organizational structure could not meet the needs of a fast-growing company. Fenghua established a new position to become an urban service provider at the end of 2018. However, the management had various opinions on how to transform the organizational structure to adapt to the new role of the company.

### 1. To Specialize or Regionalize

Fenghua has always maintained sensitivity and flexibility to the external environment for over 30 years of development. Initially, it was mainly engaged in the management of old residential properties. Later, it shifted its focus to hotel-style property management. When real estate developers from other cities rushed to the rising market in Guangzhou, Mr. Bai began to develop Fenghua's business in commercial offices and started a major transformation from a residential property service provider to an office building service provider. The latter soon became Fenghua's main business, but an oversupply of office buildings, difficulties in recovering service fees and other emerging problems pushed a second transformation from office building service provider to urban service provider. Providing urban services mainly for government buildings and public properties has become a major business of Fenghua as its share in Fenghua's business increased year by year.

Fenghua's organizational structure is giving priority to the independent development of each regional branch, combined with the coordination of functional departments and the performance assessment and management of branches and subsidiaries by the head office (see Figure 1).

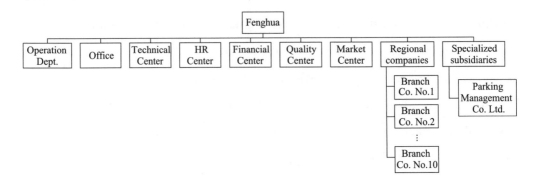

**Figure 1　Fenghua's Current Organizational Structure**

Mr. Bai, the largest shareholder of the company, was concerned that there were too many problems with the current organizational structure. With the continual growth of the number projects managed by the company year by year, the number of employees keeps increasing, and the risks confronted are also rising. If one project goes wrong, others will be affected. A specialized organizational structure is necessary. However, the current structure has many benefits and supports Fenghua's fast growth, any changes to it will increase costs and risks.

Mr. Zhao is the CEO of Fenghua. In his opinion, there is only one specialized company for parking management, while the rest are regional branch companies. It is difficult to achieve resource sharing through specialization. Moreover, employees of the regional branches are very familiar with the local markets. If specialized companies are arranged to develop the local markets, it will cause a great waste of manpower.

The third largest shareholder of FengHua, Mr. Wang had his own views. FengHua has always encouraged regional branches to actively expand the market. Personal income is closely related to the total number of projects taken, so a talent rotation machanism is hard to implement. The establishment of specialized subsidiaries allows independent business accounting and makes it clear for resource input. FengHua doesn't have a regional branch that fully focuses on one specialty. As a result, one project can be managed very differently between branches. Competition advantages on specialized service are to be improved urgently. At present, FengHua has high-costs, low profits, and it is difficult to develop value-added business. This requires FengHua to conduct in-depth specialized research on multi-mode business.

With dramatic changes in the external environment in recent years, Fenghua has become less competitive in specialization. On the one hand, many large property services companies have turned to urban public services. For example, New Century Property was positioned as an urban operation service provider; Country Garden launched the urban intergrowth plan and established strategic partnership with more than ten cities including Zunyi, Hengshui and Xichang. On the other hand, compared with internet and high-tech-based specialized companies that are small but successful and with clear market positioning, Fenghua does not have an advantage in specialized services, value-added business development, and project operation.

## 2. Brainstorm Began

It was hard for the management to reach a consensus. They decided to organize brainstorming for ideas by gathering the regional branch managers to join an open discussion, hoping that all parties would go through the pros and cons and make specific suggestions to help the management reach a conclusion.

The discussion was held as scheduled, focusing on the selection of a future organizational structure model. Mr. Bai emphasized the significance: "As our expansion goes, the original organizational structure cannot meet the needs. Scattered-site management and insufficient top-to-bottom communication limit our long-term development. Today's discussion is to select an organizational structure model that matches the market and the actual situation of our company."

Mr. Luo, the general manager of Branch Company No. 6, was the first to speak: "Our current organizational structure still has great advantages. The regionalized structure makes staff coordination very flexible. For example, office buildings are usually busy from Monday to Friday and free on weekends, while parks and scenic areas are on the opposite schedule. Therefore, we can coordinate the staffing between the two sites to reduce labor costs. As for new market development, we implement the incentive policy to let whoever applies first get first, which greatly mobilizes the enthusiasm of the branches. In addition to this advantage, regionalized development gains us a lot of experience in local markets, and it is easier to get projects …"

In contrast, Mr. Hu, the general manager of Branch Company No. 7, strongly supported specialization. He said: "The biggest obstacle is that we still use the previous management methods after our company is positioned as a urban service provider since we don't understand the new role. As a property service company without upstream real property as a support, the key for us to win the competition is specialization. It means that we need to change the original regionalized structure, which will inevitably impact existing interests."

Mr. Yang, the manager of the Parking Management Co., Ltd. stated that transferring projects of regional branch companies to specialized companies would cause problems in benefit sharing, but it was not the major difficulty in setting up specialized companies. For example, the Parking Management Company was not mature yet but the management model was relatively clear. As a specialized company, it would incur costs for providing guidance and supervision, so it may charge the regional branch companies a certain fee. So benefit sharing is not a problem as long as the overall structure is set.

Mr. Ma, the manager of Branch Company No. 3, shared his thoughts. He was against specialization. He said: "We must realize that our core members are not highly educated and most of the managers start from entry-level positions. Our company is not ready for some very big leaps without sufficient high-quality talents. Specialization requires a high management level of the company, not in line with our actual situation. We are not very specialized in either traditional property management or new urban services. Although we propose to be a city service provider, it still stays at the concept".

While the viewpoints presented by the managers have their merits, no agreement was reached on whether the company should go with a specialized or regionalized organizational structure. The current structure has both problems and advantages, and other structures have distinctive features but cannot secure desired outcomes. The discussion ended with the problem unsolved. Which organizational structure can secure the smooth development of the company?

## Questions

1. Which organizational structure corresponds to the regionalization? Which corresponds to the specialization?

2. What are the advantages and disadvantages of regionalized and specialized organizational structures?

3. What are the factors that influence the type of organizational structure?

4. If you were Mr. Bai, which organizational structure do you think better fits the development of Fenghua at the current stage? Please design a suitable organizational structure for Fenghua.

## Tips for Answering the Questions

1. There are many types of organizational structures, including functional, matrix-based, BU-based, and regional. In this case, regionalization refers to setting up the organizational departments by market scope, and specialization refers to setting up the horizontal organizational departments by business type.

【Organizational Structure and Design】

2. Each organizational structure has its advantages and disadvantages based on its features. For example, specialized organizational structure can improve efficiency, whereas a disadvantage is that it is subject to a higher bureaucratic cost.

3. There are six main factors influencing the design of organizational structure: specialization, departmentalization, chain of command, the scope of control, centralization and decentralization, and standardization.

4. Based on the influencing factors of organizational structure and the information provided in the case, an appropriate organizational structure can be designed through analysis.

# Case 10

## HR Management of NKM

## Case Description

In 2005, China reduced the export tariff on some textiles in order to promote international trading in textiles. Such measures and the relatively low labor costs in China then brought development opportunities for the companies engaged in the international trading of textiles. Considering this market opportunity, Mr. Shen Gongcan, who has worked in a textile trading company in Ningbo for more than ten years, resolutely resigned from his position as vice general manager and founded Ningbo Enkai Holdings and Export Co., Ltd. (NKM) with women's clothing as the main products. Relying on his work experience in foreign trade companies and the funds and business networking he accumulated, Shen Gongcan laid a solid foundation for his entrepreneurship. In NKM's entire development process, trading not only took lead in the development of the whole corporation, but also provided initial funds and adequate talents for its extension into other industries.

## 1. Transition from a Trading Company to a Comprehensive Corporation Integrating Trading, Production, and Training: Selecting and Cultivating Core Employees

In 2005 when it was just founded, NKM was only engaged in the business of textile trading, that is, NKM looked for potential customers and when the customer placed an order, NKM looked for factories to produce the ordered products, and then delivered the products to the customer as scheduled. In such a trading mode, NKM obtained price differences as an intermediary. Shen Gongcan was well experienced in the marketing of foreign trade, which was also the key for his team to seize the market. As a startup, NKM obtained more and more orders and realized rapid growth. In this state, NKM employed lots of salesmen to expand the foreign trade market and he started to select his core team members to cultivate them as startup partners. At this stage, NKM regarded the employees as its partners and took various measures in the management of core employees by offering development opportunities, healthy corporate culture, and well-established rules and systems.

As the company continued to grow and expand, NKM obtained more and more customers. However, in the cycle of order delivery, NKM often suffered from loss because it failed to respond to the customer needs in time as a result of misunderstanding in the communication between NKM and its factories and suppliers. In addition, all industries saw a significant rise in production costs and it would be impractical for NKM to develop rapidly further if it was still engaged in the foreign trade business only. In order to solve this problem, Shen Gongcan decided to build its own affiliated factories or partner factories as soon as possible to increase the comprehensive competitiveness of NKM. However, the management of factories differed from the management of a foreign trading company, and factories need lots of skilled workers. Shen Gongcan thought of the business model integrating "trading, production, and training", and hence he sponsored a senior workshop named "NKM Senior Workshop on Fashion" at Zhejiang Textile Vocational College. NKM arranged for the key technical workers to participate in targeted technical training free of charge. When they completed the training, they returned to the affiliated factories or partner factories of NKM to make contributions, and they also obtained higher income and HR value. In this way, a win-win mode was established in NKM: continual education of technical workers and sustainable development of NKM.

Such an integrated development mode improved NKM's ability to respond quickly to market demand. NKM has its factories, so the relevant departments could directly calculate the cost and conduct quality control. Moreover, NKM could convey its business philosophy directly to the raw materials suppliers and front-line workers, thus as guided by NKM, a healthy and stable production chain was formed among all links. With the joint efforts of the teachers from the textile college, designers of NKM, factory workers, and all upstream and downstream stakeholders, the integrated "trading, production, and training" mode became mature gradually. Highly qualified workers helped NKM obtain more development opportunities and customers and contributed to the rapid growth of NKM in the foreign trade industry of textiles.

## 2. Transition from OEM to ODM and then to OBM: Building an International Designer Team

In the initial stage, NKM mainly acted as an OEM (Original Equipment Manufacturer) in the textile trade, that is, when the customer (also the brand holder) places an order, OEM produced the products by relying upon the core technologies and design concept of the customer, and then the customer acquires all of the products and sells them with its brand. OEM mode was taken as a means for the companies in developed regions to transfer the production facilities to less developed regions to obtain greater profit margins. It also brought development opportunities for less developed regions. Although the profit and development space as an OEM was limited, it helped NKM maintain a relatively stable overall structure, obtain better experience and more development opportunities, and more important, acquire a large number of stable brand customers.

With the increase in competitors, changes in customer demands and the emergence of development expectations, many domestic trading companies began to transit from OEM to ODM (Original Design Manufacturer). Because independent design could greatly improve the comprehensive competitiveness in the industry. ODM produces the ordered products and delivers them to the customer who will sell the products with its own brand. Under the ODM mode, the manufacturer could gain more initiative and their competitiveness and bargaining power are greatly improved. The transition from OEM to ODM is not only a transformation necessary under the new trend of development, but also a wise choice of NKM in its active response to the changes in industrial development.

Product design and development capabilities are key for ODM. NKM needs to establish its own designer team. Due to its geographical location, while absorbing the influences of western culture, Turkey also absorbs eastern cultural elements and fashion and new fashion is often accepted faster than that in China. Moreover, Turkey is close to Europe. Setting up an office in Turkey is convenient for contact and communication with the customers and the exhibition halls there could show the strength of the company, which is conducive to increasing order fulfillment rates. In addition, both the salary level of designers and the rental cost of offices in Turkey are lower than those in other European countries. Considering these factors, NKM set up its first design studio in Istanbul, Turkey, and recruited local designers with European fashion experience to design products suited to European consumers. After the design, the products are manufactured by factories in China.

For foreign trade companies in the textile and clothing industry, OBM is the ultimate goal of development because both the added value and development space of OEM or ODM are very limited. When a manufacturer has its brand, its profit or comprehensive competitiveness will be greatly improved. Considering this, NKM plans to register its brand and transit towards OBM gradually by relying upon its production experience, technical innovation capacity, and other resources obtained from the development process as OEM and ODM.

### 3. Overseas Investment and Integration of Global Resources: Seeking International Business Talents

With the rise of production costs (labor, land, water and electricity) in China, NKM began to deploy its design and production resources globally. For production, it turned to Southeast Asia with low labor costs and rich raw materials. While for medium and high-end products with stringent design requirements or orders requiring fashion style and short lead time, NKM will arrange its design studio in Turkey to undertake the design and the factories in Asia to carry out production. The headquarters in China is only in charge of the allocation of global resources and coordination of relationships. The design advantages and the production advantages are both given full play.

Through such an international operation mechanism, NKM could integrate international resources and cultivate international talents to meet the demands of international development. Shen Gongcan believes that the scarcity of international talents has always constrained the growth of a foreign trade company. Compared with China, Turkey is located at the junction of Europe and Asia, where it is easier to find international designers with Western backgrounds and advanced concepts, and the products they design are more likely to meet the needs of European and American customers.

Compared with recruiting international talents to work in China by offering a much higher salary or share of project revenue, NKM set up its design studio in Turkey and established a stable team of international designers according to its needs of international talents. In addition, the designers in Turkey often communicate with Chinese designers, and their works provide a good learning channel for Chinese designers. Through such an international layout of production, design and investment, NKM has successfully integrated global resources, which has increased its profit, reduced its operating cost, and effectively improved its competitiveness.

## Questions

1. Please explain the importance of HR management to NKM.

2. How did NKM combine HR management with its strategic transformation?

3. Please describe the strategies NKM has used to retain its competent employees.

## Tips for Answering the Questions

1. There are three reasons why HR management is important. First, human resources constitute a key source of competitive advantage. Second, HR management is an integral part of organizational strategy. Third, the way that the organization treats its employees has significant impact on the performance of the organization. According to this case, we can analyze how NKM succeeded through effective HR management. The key points involved the definition, the nature and the meaning of HR.

2. According to the strategical HR management theory, we can analyze how HR management fits in the strategic transformation in NKM's three strategic transformations. For example, in the first stage, NKM regarded the core employees as its partners, and established an integrated "trade, production, and training" mode to improve the skills of technical workers, and in the second stage, NKM recruited international designers by offering high salaries. The key points involved employee recruitment and selection, compensation and welfare management, and contemporary issues of HR management.

【Retaining Competent Employees】

3. NKM pays the competent employees based on their work skills and competencies, with the evaluation of working experience, performance, occupation, industry and the company type, geographical location, profitability and size of the company. The key points involved related factors of compensation and welfare, compensation system based on competencies and skills.

# Case 11

## Leadership Practices in Wonbly

## Case Description

Hunan Wonbly Garment Co., Ltd. (hereinafter referred to as Wonbly) was founded by Luo Meiyuan in 1984. It's the first company in China that realized mass production of trousers, one of the Top 100 Competitive Enterprises in the Textile Industry of China, and one of the Top 100 Garment Enterprises in China. It is mainly engaged in the production of suits, trousers, shirts, down jackets, and windbreakers. In 2014, Liu Jiawen, the successor of Luo Meiyuan, took over the company and initiated her dream of building Wonbly into a time-honored brand by taking R&D innovation and employee motivation as the core tasks. Now under the business strategy featuring multi-brand and collectivization, it has established five brands including WONBLY GENTLEMAN (formal suits for men), WONBLY LADY (formal suit for women), WONBLY YOUNG (fashional casual e-commerce clothing for young), CHOCY (Haute Couture), and group customization.

### 1. The Founder Luo Meiyuan: Wholehearted Devotion and Sincerity

In 1984, Luo Meiyuan, who was skilled at sewing and tailoring, set up the first private garment factory in Ningxiang together with a group of skilled female workmates. At the outset, Luo Meiyuan established the culture of "seeking survival with quality, seeking development with credibility". She insisted that all products should be made elaborately to ensure excellent quality. As the manager, designer and salesman of the factory, she had to travel 40 km every day by bike between Ningxiang and Changsha for buying raw materials and then selling the finished products. With their joint efforts, this small factory was well developed and moved to a new factory ten years later. They wished the new factory have a new name. Luo Meiyuan said that the new name should be closely linked with every member of the factory. Looking back over the past, the development of the factory was indispensable from the hard work of everyone and such an experience was unforgettable for all of them. Then Wonbly was established, the pronunciation of which was similar to that of "unforgettable" in Chinese. This brand developed into a nationally renowned clothing brand.

Since 1994, Wonbly has entered a stage of rapid growth under the leadership of Luo Meiyuan, a female entrepreneur who started from scratch and often called herself uneducated modestly. She said that her management was just relying on her personality, her wholehearted devotion to the factory and her sincerity to the workmates and employees. Out of more than 800 employees of the factory, over 80% were recruited from laid-off women workers and unemployed youth. In order to encourage the employees, Luo Meiyuan often talked with them like a sister to enlighten them with her own experience and help them find their goal. When an employee made a mistake, she would talk with her over and over again to identify causes and help her to make corrections. It was called flexible management by her leadership.

In the eyes of Luo Meiyuan, a good company is similar to a good school while the employees could learn more from the daily management and the culture, and grow together with the company. Therefore, Wonbly built a staff library and an entertainment room that provided newspapers and professional books, and regularly held reading club activities for middle-level and senior executives. She required the managers to take the lead in the activities to encourage the staff to improve their knowledge as well as their professional skills, and finally to achieve a high level of comprehensive competence and innovative thoughts. Training courses for technicians were also provided by Wonbly, and that the employees could receive extensive skills training in the staff training center.

In 2014, Luo Meiyuan launched a program named "Yuan Fund", where for each piece of clothes sold by Wonbly, one yuan is donated to charity. The Fund is dedicated to supporting poor students, caring for the bereaved elderly, sponsoring the aerospace industry of China, and helping workers who have an occupational injury and victims suffering from serious natural disasters. For instance, Wonbly selects seven filial employees every year and rewards each of them with RMB 10,000. It set up a scholarship program called Wonbly-Aerospace Scholarship in cooperation with the China Space Foundation to encourage youth for aerospace technology and national defense modernization. During the last ten years, Wonbly donated food and clothes on the Double Ninth Festival for the elders of no family in the local town and helped them solve difficulties. At the end of every year, Wonbly sends a thanks letter and "red packet" to the parents of the employees to express greetings for their family support and devotion. Under the leadership of Luo Meiyuan, the employees of Wonbly are integrated with the company and feel that the company is their home.

## 2. The Successor Liu Jiawen: Let the Employees Live a Happy Life

In 2014, Liu Jiawen, daughter of Luo Meiyuan, took over the company and started the period of succession. The two leaders had distinct styles of leadership. Liu Jiawen believes that her team is mainly composed of young people who are well-educated, open-minded, and have a strong sense of innovation and personal awareness. What she needs to do is provide opportunities, cultivate their ability to undertake pressure, and assign tasks to them so that they can realize their value by completing the tasks, and thus contributing to the company. She pays attention to the spiritual and cultural needs of employees, improves the happy feelings of employees, and aims to improve their feeling of happiness, and finally achieve the goal of attracting, retaining and developing talents.

At the beginning, Liu Jiawen proposed a management structure built on equal relations with employees. It consists of three parts. First, improve the leadership mechanism of "centralized decision-making and hierarchical management" to mobilize the work enthusiasm of senior management. Second, introduce dashboard management mode into senior management. Third, all departments are required to review their work to summarize the experience, identify opportunities for improvement, work out improvement measures, and establish standardized work specifications. Liu Jiawen believes that what Wonbly offers is not only a job, but also a career, and a stage for the employees to exert their intelligence and creativity.

Liu Jiawen takes improving the happiness index of the employees of Wonbly as the fundamental means for retaining and attracting talent. For example, living facilities for young employees are provided in Wonbly according to their needs, such as a gym, yoga room and activity room. Sports meeting is held every year, and Internet access facilities are installed in the dormitory of employees. With these facilities, the mechanism of "happy learning, happy work and happy life" evolved into the cultural concept of "happy life". Only happy and energetic employees can work efficiently, make better products, and deliver better customer experience.

### 3. Epilogue: Creating a Centennial Enterprise

Under the leadership of the two generations of leaders, Wonbly has gradually grown up from a traditional manufacturing factory to a high-tech technology enterprise, from producing common clothes to delivering fashion clothes, and from an ordinary employment platform to a career platform for both employees and the company. In order to realize its vision of becoming a centennial brand, Wonbly is promoting its brand construction steadily by making quality, elegant, and satisfactory products for customers.

## *Questions*

1. Based on the leadership practices in Wonbly, describe why managers should become leaders.

2. According to Maslow's theory, what needs are met by founder Luo Meiyuan's "wholehearted devotion and sincerity" leadership style and the successor Liu Jiawen's "let employees live a happy life" leadership style respectively?

3. According to the leadership contingency theory, why did the successor change her leadership style when Luo Meiyuan has achieved success with charismatic leadership?

## Tips for Answering the Questions

1. Managers should be leaders because leaders can influence others and have the power of management. Leadership refers to the things to be done by a leader, which is a process that the leader leads and influences a team to achieve its goals. It can be seen from this case that the two generations of leaders became different types of leaders according to their respective personalities, but the similarity of them is that they both pay attention to tasks and personnel. The leaders of both generations of the company can consider about the needs of the employees and take the interests of the employees as a key issue of their decision-making, which has won the support and love of the employees, and finally make the employees complete the organizational tasks efficiently. The key points include the definition of leader and the importance of leader.

2. Maslow believes that people have five levels of needs, namely physiological needs, safety-security needs, social-belongingness needs, esteem needs, and self-actualization needs. Maslow believes that each level of needs must be substantially satisfied before the next level can be activated. Leaders should determine the level of needs of employees, and then take corresponding measures to motivate employees to work hard to achieve their needs. For example, Luo Meiyuan focuses on satisfying the social-belongingness needs of employees, while Liu Jiawen focuses more on satisfying the self-actualization needs of employees.

【Hierarchy of Needs Theory】

3. According to leadership contingency theory, task-oriented leadership perform best in extremely favorable and extremely unfavorable situations, while relationship-oriented leadership perform best in moderately favorable situations. For this case, we can discuss the relationship between task-oriented leadership and relationship-oriented leadership styles, and analyze their leadership traits.

# Case 12

## Entrepreneurial Team of Lituo Energy

## Case Description

How to organize and set up a professional entrepreneurial team for a startup company? How to improve the efficiency of the entrepreneurial team? For these issues, Chen Du, founder of Lituo Energy, had already had her answers before starting her adventure in the new energy business. She hoped to organize a professional entrepreneurial team to conduct research in and promote the application of biomass energy. In the past three years, Chen Du has led her core R&D team to break through traditional technical bottlenecks and successfully transformed agricultural and forestry wastes such as straw and sawdust into renewable biomass energy that can replace petroleum-based fuels, including biodiesel, heavy oil, bio-asphalt, bio-carbon materials, etc., which can help to achieve those almost impossible goals in the new energy industry at present at a relatively low cost with remarkable economic and environmental benefits.

### 1. Finding an Entrepreneurial Project

At the beginning of the 21st century, due to people's growing awareness of environmental issues, environmental protection slogans could be seen everywhere on the street. Under the influence of this atmosphere, an idea of "environmental protection" took root and germinated in Chen Du's heart when she was still a primary school student. Chen Du has a great passion for environmental protection. When she was an undergraduate student, she often climbed mountains with her classmates to pick up garbage, and always hoped to have the opportunity to participate in a United Nations public welfare project.

When she studied at the University of California, Chen Du learned that biomass energy was a common technology industry in North America, but it has not been fully industrialized in China. If existing technologies can be integrated and parameters can be adjusted for China's specific raw materials, a large number of agricultural and forestry wastes in China will become substitutes for petrochemical resources. It's a potential market opportunity. Chen Du became aware of a new technology of biomass energy at the university. Chen Du had the idea to establish a biomass energy company that can satisfy the need to protect the environment and generate profits.

The new technology of biomass energy was developed by a professor at the University of California. Considering the potential of the technology, many companies came to seek cooperation as soon as it was released. How to compete with those competitors and obtain the chance to use the technology is undoubtedly a huge challenge for Chen Du. Chen Du believed that entrepreneurial projects would not come to her spontaneously, and she must take the initiative to fight for them. Taking advantage of the colleague relationship, Chen Du repeatedly visited and communicated with the professor. However, the professor had a lot of doubts because international cooperation was not easy. Chen Du told the professor about her childhood dream of environmental protection and her wish to establish a clean energy enterprise in China to make greater contributions to society. Deeply moved by Chen Du, the professor finally agreed to join her project.

## 2. Building the Team

However, having only technology is far from enough. A professional team is the key to the success of a business. Chen Du is very good at expressing herself, and she has never been afraid of meeting and communicating with leaders from large enterprises. With her efforts, she finally obtained an investment of RMB10 million. Meanwhile, she invited a good team of high-level talents with overseas backgrounds with her excellent social skills, and built a world-class international team for Lituo Energy. Within the team, there were American technical experts specializing in biotechnology research and organic chemistry, the chief engineer who had been fully engaged in the R&D of chemical technology for over 20 years, as well as professionals who were familiar with marketing and service of new energy products. In 2017, Chen Du graduated from the university and returned to China, with the latest biomass conversion technology and her R&D team, and founded Lituo Energy.

As a start-up, Lituo Energy has "weaknesses" in both technology and management, but Chen Du's excellent leadership and the cooperation ability of the team have brought vitality to this start-up. Majored in mathematics at the university, Chen Du had a solid professional foundation, and was very familiar with the knowledge of data models, economic models. The refining and recycling of new energy materials need to be supported by an accurate mixing ratio. Prior to energy refining, she would first build the preliminary architecture based on her professional knowledge and input different experimental data into the architecture. These core technologies later became the core competitive advantages of the enterprise. In the process of project implementation, different cultural backgrounds did not become an obstacle, but became a source for local engineers and foreign engineers to inspire each other with new ideas. Chen Du respected the opinions and suggestions of these professionals. The team kept efficient communication during the critical technology breakthroughs, made decisions together, and solved a series of technical problems.

The goal of Chen Du and her team has always been to contribute to the environmental protection. They hope to develop competitive clean energy in the market that can replace the high-cost and heavy-polluting petrochemical products, and take the lead in parameter regulation. The common goal greatly stimulated the passion of the team. For example, the team members always worked overnight for several days to monitor the data to prevent errors in the operation process. All of them worked together to achieve the goal of refining petroleum biochar with higher added value from biomass energy.

The long-term efforts of the team have paid off. Up to now, the pilot-scale operation process and material conversion rate in Taizhou plant have worked well, and in terms of designated equipment involvement and process control measures, they have established a unique biochar process package and database, which can meet the conditions for large-scale production of biomass fuel and small-scale production of petroleum biochar. The future products of Lituo Energy can be applied to graphite electrodes and graphite negative electrode materials for lithium-ion battery, both of which are high value-added and highly demanded in the market, and are also the materials that Lituo Energy's team desires to obtain after repeated business model optimization and technical R&D adjustment.

### 3. Epilogue

Looking back at their entrepreneurial experience, Chen Du believes that human resources are the core competitiveness. The goal of Lituo Energy in the next stage is to introduce capital, support pilot production and trial cooperation, and conduct mass production through technical export or collaborative factory to push the company's products from the pilot stage to the industrialization stage.

## Questions

1. Based on this case, analyze what preparations the founder made to form the team.

2. From this case, what are the characteristics of the entrepreneurial team?

3. How did the founder improve the efficiency of the entrepreneurial team?

## Tips for Answering the Questions

1. Based on the theories of leadership traits, we can analyze the founder's preparations from the aspects of personal ability, personality and environmental impact. For example, the founder of Lituo Energy spent a lot of time, carried out repeated investigations to select the project and finally selected the project based on her interest and existing opportunity. Furthermore, the entrepreneur needs to identify the stage that the team is currently in, as each stage involves different matters and activities. For example, the formation of a team is the first stage of team development. The entrepreneur needs to attract the members to join the team and define the goal, structure and leadership of the team. The key points involve team management, team development stages, etc.

2. The characteristics of an entrepreneurial team include sharing leadership roles, assuming

both individual responsibilities and team responsibilities, having specific goals, completing work collectively, open discussions in conferences, evaluating performance based on the work results of the team, and having work decided and completed by all members together. In the case of Lituo Energy, the entrepreneurial team kept win-win cooperation, open communication and joint decision-making under the complex international background. The key points involved team characteristics, influencing factors of team performance, etc.

3. The methods to improve the efficiency of entrepreneurial teams include a powerful leader being in charge of the team, the members being assigned individual responsibilities, the team goals being consistent with the organizational goals, the members completing the tasks independently, high-efficiency meetings, tasks decided by the team leader and then assigned to team members. This problem can be analyzed from the aspects of professional talent recruitment and team management, etc. The key points involve team characteristics and vision, team goals, role allocation of team members, etc.

【Team Effectiveness】

# Case 13

## The Motivation for Store Managers at Ningbo Haichen Pharmacy

## Case Description

In 1999, Ms. Xu, graduated from a vocational school, occasionally found a clerical job in a pharmaceutical factory in Jinan, and thus entered the pharmaceutical industry. Because of her outstanding performance, Xu was transferred to the sales department two years later. In 2003, Xu was appointed to Ningbo Kaixinren Pharmacy as a counter salesperson.

The Kaixinren Pharmacy was the first pharmacy in Ningbo to adopt an open-shelf purchasing model. Working in the Kaixinren Pharmacy, Xu not only learned sales skills but also gained a very deep understanding of consumer behavior in pharmacies. More importantly, she began to observe the business model and management characteristics of the pharmacy. After getting a clear picture of the operation in the pharmaceutical industry, Xu had an idea to open her own business.

In 2010, Xu's husband retired from a military, and the couple decided to start their own business, Ningbo Haichen Pharmacy. Thanks to Xu's years of sales experience in the pharmaceutical industry and the couple's hard work, they soon achieved profitability.

### 1. Selecting Store Managers

In 2014, the couple had their fourth store. However, at this moment, Xu and her husband began to feel overwhelmed and failed to make strict quality control and management tracking on each store from time to time. In the actual operation, when the manager was not working on-site, employees often falsely reported the operating revenue. It was impossible for Xu to always be on-site, nor could she remind employees not to make false reports every day, which would make employees feel distrusted and disrespected and eventually quit the job. Finding qualified store managers and effectively motivating them to manage pharmacies had been a top priority.

A pharmacy must be equipped with at least one professional pharmacist and one assistant pharmacist. Then, according to the size and passenger flow, the storekeeper could decide to hire salespersons, cashiers, and store managers for better operation. Many small stores often had altogether two pharmacists who served also as the cashier and the store manager respectively. Sales ability was the core competitiveness of a store manager. A salesperson with qualified pharmacy knowledge and good sales skills could increase the final sales amount by 3-5 times the planned. Moreover, in retail pharmacies, female employees had natural advantages compared to male employees. In most cases, female employees were better at recommending medicines. Therefore, almost all the store managers selected by Xu were hardworking women.

## 2. Employee Incentives

Xu and her husband adopted a very flexible plan. They set a baseline sales amount based on the original annual sales. Employees could get a basic salary if they reached the baseline sales amount. Furthermore, employees would earn a proportional commission for the part that exceeded the baseline sales, which encouraged them to work harder and improve performance. Moreover, they reduced the number of employees without affecting sales. For example, if the number of employees was reduced from three to two, then the wages of three employees would be paid to two employees. Since the two employees left could earn more, the original baseline sales would also be increased correspondingly. Therefore, the total wages would be a little lower. This plan could result in a decrease in enterprise costs and an improvement in employee salaries, target index, and employee motivation.

## 3. Unique Store Manager Contracting Model

In addition, Xu created a unique contracting model to motivate the store managers. For example, for a store that could earn 200,000 yuan per year, Xu would bear the rent and equip the store with one licensed pharmacist and one assistant pharmacist. If the licensed pharmacist finally became the store manager, he or she would be responsible for daily expenses, and Xu took the expected profits of 200,000 yuan at the end of the year. The rest of the profits would go to the store manager. However, there was a problem: every pharmacy needs a certain amount of inventory to maintain the daily operation, but most of the store managers did not have the financial means to purchase the store. If the inventory was completely controlled by the store manager instead of Xu, the store manager might sell the inventory and take the money away.

Xu solved this problem using "installment". For instance, if the inventory was valued at 100,000 yuan on the day of contracting, the store manager could complete the contract in half a year in installments. In the first 6 months of the contract, Xu would be paid 10,000−20,000 yuan with monthly sales. This not only alleviated Xu's concerns about the intentional disappearance of the store manager but also provided start-up funds for the store manager. Meanwhile, the installment also increased the store manager's breach of contract costs, encouraging them to operate more conscientiously.

When the store manager ended the contract for unexpected reasons, Xu would also purchase the inventory back in "installments" taking half a year. In this way, Xu could always take the initiative and encourage the contractor to strive for increasing the revenue while ensuring that the inventory would not be maliciously transferred. This kind of contracting model had been implemented by Xu in three pharmacies for four years, and the result had always been especially good. The performance of the three pharmacies improved significantly. Xu achieved the expected return every year, and the financial situation of the three store managers improved significantly.

## 4. New Challenges for the Contracting Model under Dynamic Industry Changes

(1) Profit Squeezed by Competition Among Individual Pharmacies

Ningbo had a high proportion of individual pharmacies. Before 2020, this number was as high as 60%−70%. The reason for this situation was historical. The owners of individual pharmacies in Ningbo mostly worked as licensed pharmacists in the supply and marketing cooperatives. They had professional knowledge and excellent interpersonal relationships with hospitals and pharmaceutical companies. Accordingly, after the restructuring of the supply and marketing cooperatives, they took over the business as self-employed operators. Since the self-employed business model was relatively flexible, pharmacies based on self-employed business model had been prosperous in Ningbo. However, the large number of individual pharmacies has led to fierce price competition. As a result, the profit margins have been reduced in recent years. When the price of a medicine in a pharmacy drops, almost all pharmacies will follow. For example, the purchase price of Ganmaoling granule (a Chinese herbal medication) is 8.5 yuan. In a normal situation, the retail price of this medicine will be increased by 10%—15% based on the purchase price, namely selling for 9.35—9.78 yuan. However, this medicine might be discounted to 4.8 yuan in Ningbo pharmacies which lose 3.7 yuan for every box sold. That is because Ningbo pharmacies usually make a profit by attracting consumers with the low price of selected medicines and then guiding them to buy high-margin medicines. More and more medicines are shown in abnormal low-price-list to attract consumers on condition of intensive competition. The dramatic decline in profit makes the original goals hard to be achieved. So the original contracting model is not as effective as it used to be.

(2) Medical Insurance Reform Further Compressed the Surviving Space of Individual Pharmacies

Medical insurance reform will enlarge the market size in the medical industry finally. Putting appointed medicines for common diseases on the medical reimbursement list, separating medicine prescribing and dispensing may be good for a pharmacy in the long run. However, not all patients will prefer to purchase medicine prescribed in a pharmacy. Moreover, the government's subsidy allows hospital pharmacies to set prices without added profit, while individual pharmacies with no subsidy have to pay rent, taxes, fees, etc. The price advantages of individual pharmacies no longer exist.

(3) Pharmacy Chain Operations Is Becoming a Trend

Due to the special nature of the industry, the government has strict regulations on the pharmaceutical industry. For regulatory agencies, managing a large number of individual pharmacies is very costly, while it is relatively easy to regulate chain pharmacies with standardized operating procedures. Government regulators are supportive of the chain operation of pharmacies. According to the data of the China Medical Products Administration Statistic Report, as of June 2021, the number of nationwide pharmacies is 586,000, an increase of 139,000 from 2016, of which chain pharmacies increased by 115,000. Faced with such industrial trends, Xu's stores are also under the pressure of restructuring to chain pharmacies. After the chain operation, the purchase right of pharmacies will be transferred to the head office, and the store manager will no longer have the purchase right at all. Therefore, will the store manager contracting model adopted by Xu still be an effective motivation? If not, what kind of motivation should she choose?

## Questions

1. What are the major motivation issues in the pharmaceutical retail industry according to Maslow's hierarchy of needs theory?

2. Using one or more motivation theories, explain why Xu's store manager contracting model can well motivate the store manager.

3. Under the new changes in the industry, what challenges will Xu's store manager contracting model face? How should Xu motivate them?

## Tips for Answering the Questions

1. According to Maslow's hierarchy of needs theory, the motivation issues at play span various levels of needs. For example, physiological needs are not met when employees are not getting satisfactory salaries, social needs are not met when staying in the store alone the whole day, esteem needs are not met because of the inability to get promotions.

2. This case can be analyzed from the perspective of employee motivation. The theories that might be involved include the need theory of Maslow, the two-factor theory, the goal-setting theory, the fair theory, etc.

【Goal-setting Theory】

3. This case should be discussed from the perspective of the impact of new external environmental changes upon the enterprise's operations, and it should be emphasized that environmental changes will force companies to make corresponding adjustments to their employee motivation methods. In this case, the previous monetary ways of motivating store managers might not be effective. Because the head office standardizes the whole process of operation, which leaves very limited margin for store managers. Non-monetary ways of motivation should be considered, such as providing employees with a better way of working and a better work environment, providing opportunities for skill development, etc.

# Case 14

# Leadership Practices of Chambroad

## Case Description

Shandong Chambroad Holdings Co., Ltd. (hereinafter referred to as Chambroad) is a large private enterprise that operates in multiple fields, such as petrochemicals, fine chemicals, and modern agriculture. Regarding traditional Confucian culture as the source of enterprise management, Chambroad has established a corporate culture system with delivering satisfactory products to the customers and cultivating talents that benefit the society as its mission, and benevolence and filial piety as its core. Under the leadership of Ma Yunsheng, the Chairman, Chambroad has won many honors, such as the Outstanding Enterprise in Contract Performance and Credibility, Outstanding Enterprise in Corporate Culture Building, and Top 500 Chinese Enterprises.

### 1. Benevolence and Filial Piety, the Foundation of the Corporate Culture

Ma Yunsheng, the Chairman of Chambroad, regards corporate culture as the soul of an enterprise. He advises that Chinese enterprises should create a corporate culture with characteristics based on traditional Chinese culture, and mechanically copying the management concepts of western countries is unwise. In the opinion of Ma Yunsheng, the managers of enterprises should comprehend and put into practice the management methods and skills based on and as guided by culture, and Chinese enterprises need to learn from and be empowered by Chinese culture to compete with and surpass others. By conducting a study on "Industrial Development and Building of Social Enterprise, Application of Chinese Culture in Enterprise Management" and taking Chinese traditional culture as the origin of enterprise management, Ma Yunsheng is committed to building Chambroad into an enterprise that is more responsible and more beneficial for the society, establishing the corporate culture system based on benevolence and filial piety, and fostering the management culture with Chinese wisdom.

### 2. Altruism Makes Chambroad Succeed

From the perspective of Confucianism, management may be considered a process of understanding and influencing the psychological activities of employees, and the desirable effects may be achieved only when the employees are "moved with emotion". On this basis, Ma Yunsheng proposes that the operation and management practices of Chambroad should be based on the following principles: respecting humanity, winning the heart and mind, managing behavior, controlling the risks, and meeting the needs. According to these principles, managers must treat employees with benevolence and communicate with the employees sincerely. Benevolence means being considerate of others and treating others generously. The managers must be conscientious and grateful in the management of an enterprise. Only altruism could make the enterprise succeed.

Chambroad draws wisdom from the Chinese traditional culture. It values the role of spiritual contracts. It believes that when the enterprise reaches a "spiritual contract" with the employees, management can rely on the moral level and self-discipline of individual employees. For example, the reimbursement of expenditures in Chambroad is a trust and self-discipline process. The employees are only needed to make applications on the intranet of Chambroad, and then get reimbursed by submitting the relevant invoices or proofs to the financial department. Any signature of managers is not required, instead, they are only required to read the honesty pledge on the wall and promise to be responsible for their actions. In this way, the employees are given trust and encouraged to act honestly. They could feel that they are trusted, and in turn, they will also work for the enterprise sincerely. Such a mutually beneficial interaction between employees and the enterprise has greatly improved the efficiency of reimbursement.

Ma Yunsheng often says that Chambroad is not his own business, it's a family of all employees who works for Chambroad. In Chambroad, all employees are family. Ma Yunsheng believes that the health of the employees is the most. Nowadays, sub-health has gradually become a problem for numerous adults who sit in the office for long hours and deal with frequent social intercourse activities. To protect the health of employees, Chambroad organizes quarterly physical examinations for all employees. Chambroad also issues a prohibition of Alcohol to prohibit drinking on working days. Once at a reception dinner,

Ma Yunsheng drank alcohol. After he returned to the company, he first apologized to all employees and then paid 300,000 yuan as a fine. Thereafter, the prohibition of alcohol was thoroughly implemented in Chambroad. Many employees of Chambroad said that they had to participate in frequent entertainment activities before. After the prohibition of alcohol was issued, they had more time to stay at home to build more harmonic relations with the family. Besides, they had more time to exercise and participate in other cultural and sports activities, and their physical condition has improved greatly. These rules and requirements of Chambroad represent not only the responsibilities and commitments of the employees to Chambroad but also the care and responsibility of Chambroad towards each employee.

## 3. Employees Are Required to Love Their Parents, Enterprise, and Country

In the process of development of Chambroad, Ma Yunsheng has incorporated the culture of filial piety into the management concept. To foster the atmosphere of filial piety, Chambroad created the filial piety subsidy system in 2007 to grant filial piety subsidies every month to employees whose parents are aged over 70. To put the filial piety subsidy system into practice, Chambroad opened special deposit cards on the theme of Taishan-Chambroad Filial Piety Culture with Boxing Rural Cooperative Bank. These deposit cards are opened in the name of the parents of the employees and are specially used for the payment of filial piety subsidies. The parents of qualified employees receive filial piety subsidies every month. To put the filial piety subsidy system into practice, Chambroad opened special deposit cards on the theme of Taishan-Chambroad Filial Piety Culture with Boxing Rural Cooperative Bank. These deposit cards are opened in the name of the parents of the employees and are specially used for the payment of filial piety subsidies. The parents of qualified employees receive filial piety subsidies every month. In 2014, Chambroad also established the Loyalty and Filial Piety Rewards system to issue rewards to the parents of the employees who had worked for Chambroad for over 20 years, as a recognition of the employees who have worked with Chambroad for years. In the opinion of Ma Yunsheng, subsidies and rewards are not the purposes, they are only the means taken by Chambroad to express gratitude for the families of the employees. Chambroad wishes to create a physically and mentally pleasant living environment for the employees during their hours off work. Chambroad has rooted the benevolence and filial piety culture into the bloodstream of the enterprise. Relying upon such corporate culture, Chambroad wishes to build the core values of loving parents, enterprise, and country and establish a team that is caring, responsible, moral, and grateful to society. Ma Yunsheng believes that as long as a healthy corporate culture is established, Chambroad will undoubtedly grow and expand. Chambroad is committed to enhancing each employee's sense of social responsibility, building a team that is loving, courageous, conscientious and actively give back to society.

## 4. Epilogue

Among the numerous successful entrepreneurs, only a few of them like Ma Yunsheng successfully built the corporate culture into a gold standard. The benevolence and filial piety of Chambroad not only reflected the excellent traditional culture of China but also showed the wisdom and cultural background of the entrepreneur. Upholding the concept of "serving the country and society with industry", Chambroad combines the wisdom of Chinese culture with the management practices learned from western countries, establishes a management mode featuring Chinese wisdom, and builds a warm atmosphere for the employees. It has created a unique and thought-provoking way to succeed in the development of enterprise.

## *Questions*

1. Based on the case, analyze what the role of the leader is.

2. Based on the Charismatic/Visionary Leadership Theory, analyze the leadership style of Ma Yunsheng.

3. According to Herzberg's Two-Factor Theory, analyze how Ma Yunsheng motivates the enthusiasm of the employees.

## Tips for Answering the Questions

1. Firstly, an excellent leader should determine the development direction of the enterprise and identify what is right, when, and who should be assigned to a certain work. In this case, Ma Yunsheng takes benevolence and filial piety as the foundation of its development concept. Secondly, the leader should work out regulations and rules for the enterprise to specify clearly what is advocated and what is banned. It must be noted that the leader needs to set an example through his conduct because he is often imitated by the employees. In this case, Ma Yunsheng set a good example in the implementation of the prohibition of alcohol. Finally, the leader should motivate the enthusiasm of employees by establishing trusty and cooperative relationships with them to make them work more efficiently. In this case, Ma Yunsheng cares about the health of employees and grants subsidies to the parents of the employees, which has not only gained the respect and support of the employees but also improved their work efficiency greatly.

2. A charismatic leader is enthusiastic and confident, influences others with his personal qualities, and conducts himself in a specific way. A visionary leader establishes and conveys a feasible, trusty, and attractive vision that could improve the current conditions. The vision is very appealing and inspiring once it is properly defined and implemented, and could become true by gathering all possible skills, talents, and resources. In this case, Ma Yunsheng advocates the benevolence and filial piety culture, treats the employees in an altruistic manner, and inspires the employees to be honest and responsible. As the employees accept the leadership of Ma Yunsheng, the cohesion of Chambroad is very strong. Such a way of leadership helps improve the performance of the enterprise.

3. According to Herzberg's Two-Factor Theory, intrinsic motivation factors are related to job satisfaction, while extrinsic hygiene factors are associated with dissatisfaction. Hygiene factors and motivation factors are independent and vary greatly from each other. Hygiene factors just prevent dissatisfaction, but will not motivate. Motivation factors are motivational to the employees

【Two-factor Theory】

because they could feel intrinsic rewards. The enterprise must value the motivation factors to inspire the employees to work hard because these factors are intrinsic and necessary for improving employee satisfaction. In this case, the employees are given adequate trust in the work. For example, the signature of the superior is not required for reimbursement, the parents of employees are granted subsidies, and Chambroad is advocated as a family of all employees instead of a private enterprise of the Chairman. Due to these factors, the employees are very satisfied with the work and the work efficiency is high.

# Case 15

## JF's Control and Management Practice

## *Case Description*

JF is a company that manufactures and sells kitchen and bathroom household products made of stainless steel and wood. It has strong capabilities in manufacturing, cost control, design, and development, and has been implementing and improving its quality management system and social responsibility system. In recent years, JF, as an OEM, provides about 86 percent of its products to IKEA. JF is IKEA's production base of stainless-steel household products in East China, and one of the few best-known suppliers of IKEA in Asia. JF Furnishings' impressive achievements are inextricably linked with its good control practice.

**1. Risk Control through Checks and Balances**

JF is jointly owned by Bao Jisheng, Bao Xiangqian (son of Bao Jisheng), and a partner from Hong Kong. The Hong Kong partner holds 55 percent of JF's shares, but does not participate in the day-to-day management of the company and only participates in the decision-making on major issues. Bao Xiangqian and his father hold a 45 percent stake, and Bao Xiangqian takes charge of JF's day-to-day management. This unique governance structure model is related to the experience of Bao Xiangqian, the actual controller of JF. Bao Xiangqian has strong entrepreneurial passion and capability but lacks awareness of risk control. The partner in Hong Kong is widely known as a rational businessperson with rich experience in financial decision-making and risk control, and recognizes Bao Xiangqian's management ability. The partner is a good external restraint on the risk-taking behavior of Bao Xiangqian.

Choosing a complementary partner and diluting the company's equity to reduce the decision-making risks is a deliberate decision made by the first generation of JF. To this end, the family offered 55 percent of their shares to the Hong Kong partner and retained 45 percent of the shares and the power of management. The advantage of this model is that the annual reports and important plans are submitted to the shareholders' meeting for deliberation, and the Hong Kong partner can put forward advice and suggestions to the management and is entitled to a veto over critical issues. The family management represented by Bao Xiangqian is in charge of the day-to-day management of JF, including monitoring, comparison, and correction of performance, and implementation plans and controls. Such a shareholding structure creates checks and balances between the investor and the management.

**2. Learning by Doing**

In 1998, Bao Xiangqian's father founded JF Stainless Steel Company to undertake a local sheet metal business. In 1999, Bao Xiangqian got an order from IKEA for 100,000 stainless-steel trash cans. The order was far beyond his father's expectations. An IKEA supplier must be able to provide products of high quality but low prices, but at that time, the factory only had a footprint of 500 square meters, and its production capacity was not sufficient. Both their technology and venue could not meet IKEA's requirements. In addition, Bao Xiangqian's father thought it was almost impossible to achieve breakeven according to IKEA's offer, and strongly opposed the order. However, Bao Xiangqian thought IKEA was a good customer, and even if the order did not make a profit, IKEA may place large orders in the future. He had many rounds of negotiations with the procurement manager of IKEA. In the end, Bao Xiangqian convinced his father to take the order, and they began cooperation with IKEA. Fortunately, the fluctuation of the economy in that year led to a decrease in the raw material price, so this order was breakeven. Hereafter, IKEA's orders came one after another, proving Bao Xiangqian's capability to his father and the Hong Kong partner. Then Bao Xiangqian became a member of JF's top management and a co-founder.

In 2005, IKEA's orders could not satisfy the needs of JF, which just went public and needed rapid growth. So JF offered to produce wooden furniture for IKEA. IKEA asked JF to produce samples for a product series within three months and compete with other candidate suppliers. JF immediately mobilized the team, bought a full set of costly equipment and raw materials, and independently completed the whole process from R&D to production of the samples. The competitive bidding of IKEA took place in Shanghai.

The products of JF were superior to those of other candidate suppliers, but its qualification was inferior. Bao Xiangqian suggested IKEA conduct a blind review where executives of IKEA chose samples without knowing the supplier names. Finally, JF won four votes in the blind review and was awarded the contract for wooden furniture. The new order and equity financing gave an impetus to the great-leap-forward development of JF. In just one year, JF completed the upgrade from a stainless-steel factory to a standardized, modern factory that can also produce wooden furniture.

In 2007, with better cost control, JF turned its eyes to the cellular board business, which represented the leading furniture technology of IKEA and was once only awarded to IKEA's wholly-owned subsidiaries. To achieve the goal, JF optimized its control approach according to the technology differences, and invested heavily in technology R&D. Finally, they developed four breakthrough technologies including replacing paint with stickers, shortening cold pressing time, sealing package of table feet, and designing the wood frame, and greatly reduced the cost of cellular board furniture. Such a breakthrough convinced IKEA of JF's capability and helped JF win cellular board furniture orders from IKEA, giving JF a unique position in IKEA's entire supplier system.

## 3. Great Success from Lean Control

JF has been constantly seeking breakthroughs in technology innovations and streamlining its control and management to improve operational performance. On the one hand, technological innovations contribute to the highest profit growth at the lowest cost and are therefore considered as the best performance growth driver. Lean entrepreneurship embodies JF's technology and management approach developed through years of cooperation with IKEA. With this approach, JF's technology personnel pursue both simplicity and quality in the design and development of products. The iconic cellular board technology is exactly the result of JF's relentless pursuit of better process control and technology innovations.

On the other hand, JF sets the production over-fulfillment and quality rewards to motivate employees through performance incentives, which is the only performance management mode established by JF. On the premise of satisfactory quality, the Finance Director calculates the breakeven point based on JF's current product mix, and the sales corresponding to this breakeven point will be used as the basis for determining the production over-fulfillment reward. The excess amount, after deducting the fixed expenses of the company, will be given to the employees as a bonus. On the contrary, if something goes wrong with a certain department, affecting the production, all people may lose their production over-fulfillment rewards of that month. The breakeven point is updated every three years. As to the weighting of different departments, JF assigns a weight to each department according to the weighted average of recommendations proposed by all departments. This ensures fairness and objectivity. As the yield is linked to their interests, all employees are very concerned about the products every month, all departments supervise each other, and all people work hard towards the same goal of performance growth. Besides, the annual employee turnover of JF is only 5 percent around.

Bao Xiangqian believes that the best control is to establish a "clean" operation mode and simple rules, leaving no room for argument among employees. In this way, employees can focus on production, and align their behaviors with the performance goals. In his entrepreneurial journey, Bao Xiangqian identifies the most valuable parts of other management systems and integrates them into his own business. He uses the least amount of resources to do what he wants to do, never stops innovation with a lean philosophy, and controls risks with the optimal governance structure.

## *Questions*

1. What kind of control measures behaviors were used by JF? What are the achievements? Please analyze the importance of control to the organization based on the case study.

2. According to this case, analyze how enterprises need to adjust the organizational structure to achieve financial control?

3. According to this case, analyze how JF measures organizational performance.

## Tips for Answering the Questions

1. Controlling is to measure the actual performance, compare it with the standard, and correct deviations. The importance of control lies in: ①It is the only way for managers to know whether the goal has been achieved and why the goal has not been achieved; ②It provides necessary information and feedback that can give managers confidence in delegating power;

【What Is Controlling and Why Is It Important?】

③It helps protect the organization and its assets. The control standard is the goal set by managers at the planning stage. From this case, we can see that JF focuses on two goals, over-fulfillment production and quality assurance, it sets standards around these goals, and helps its employees understand and take the initiative to fulfill the goals. We may understand the importance and control standards from how to set management goals. The key points include the definition, criteria, and importance of controlling.

2. Contemporary controlling issues need to consider specific scenarios, for example, building a specific family governance structure to control performance. In this case, JF implements financial control through co-governance by the family and an external financial investor to avoid decision-making mistakes and hence performance problems, such as reducing risks of critical decisions by analyzing the financial report and setting financial measurement standards. The key points include financial control and organizational structure.

3. Managers need appropriate tools to monitor and measure organizational performance, which represents the cumulative results of all activities in the organization. Commonly used measures of organizational performance include: ①Productivity, that is, the total output of products or services divided by the total input to produce these outputs; ②Organizational effectiveness, which is a measure of the suitability and realization of the organization's goals; ③Industry and company rankings issued by commercial publications. In this case,

we can understand how to measure organizational performance and control employee behavior through the production over-fulfillment and quality rewards set by JF. The key points include organizational performance and productivity.